MODERN WARS
THE HUMANITARIAN CHALLENGE

A REPORT FOR THE INDEPENDENT COMMISSION
ON INTERNATIONAL HUMANITARIAN ISSUES

Presented by Mohammed Bedjaoui
Foreword by Pierre Graber

Modern Wars

Modern Wars

The Humanitarian Challenge

A Report for the Independent Commission on International Humanitarian Issues

Zed Books Ltd.
London and New Jersey

This report does not necessarily reflect the views, individually or collectively, of the members of the Independent Commission on International Humanitarian Issues (ICIHI). It is based on research carried out for ICIHI and was prepared under the supervision of its Secretariat with the guidance of the ICIHI Working Group on Humanitarian Norms and Armed Conflicts.

Modern Wars was first published by Zed Books Ltd.,
57 Caledonian Road, London N1 9BU and
171 First Avenue, Atlantic Highlands, New Jersey 07716, in 1986.

© Secretariat of the Independent Commission on International
Humanitarian Issues, 1986

Cover design by Henry Iles
Cover picture: 'The dove and peace' by Pablo Picasso, 10 May 1962
Copyright © 1986 by PRO LITTERIS, Zurich, and SPADEM, Paris
Typeset by Grassroots Typeset, London
Printed and bound in Great Britain by Biddles of Guildford

British Library Cataloguing in Publication Data

Modern Wars: the humanitarian challenge: a report.
1. War (International Law)
I. Independent Commission on International
Humanitarian Issues
341.6   JX4511

ISBN 0-86232-694-X
ISBN 0-86232-695-8 Pbk

Contents

The Independent Commission on International Humanitarian Issues

Co-Chairmen:

Sadruddin Aga Khan (Iran) Hassan bin Talal (Jordan)

Members:

Susanna Agnelli	(Italy)
Talal Bin Abdul Aziz Al Saud	(Saudi Arabia)
Paulo Evaristo Arns, Vice-Chairman	(Brazil)
Mohammed Bedjaoui	(Algeria)
Henrik Beer, Treasurer	(Sweden)
Luis Echeverria Alvarez	(Mexico)
Pierre Graber	(Switzerland)
Ivan Head	(Canada)
M. Hidayatullah	(India)
Aziza Hussein	(Egypt)
Manfred Lachs	(Poland)
Robert McNamara	(USA)
Lazar Mojsov	(Yugoslavia)
Mohamed Mzali, Vice-Chairman	(Tunisia)
Sadako Ogata, Vice-Chairman	(Japan)
David Owen	(United Kingdom)
Willibald P. Pahr, Vice-Chairman	(Austria)
Shridath S. Ramphal	(Guyana)
Ru Xin	(China)
Salim A. Salim	(Tanzania)
Léopold Sédar Senghor	(Senegal)
Soedjatmoko	(Indonesia)
Desmond Tutu	(South Africa
Simone Veil	(France)
Gough Whitlam	(Australia)

Secretary General, ex-officio member:

Zia Rizvi (Pakistan)

Other ICIHI Reports*

FAMINE: A Man-Made Disaster? (Pan Books, London/Sydney, 1985). Other language editions: Arabic, French, Italian, Japanese, Portuguese, Serbo-Croatian, Spanish and Urdu.

STREET CHILDREN: A Growing Urban Tragedy (Weidenfeld & Nicolson, London, 1986). Other language editions: Arabic, French, Indonesian, Japanese, Serbo-Croatian and Spanish.

THE ENCROACHING DESERT: The Consequences of Human Failure (Zed Books, London/New Jersey, 1986 and College Press, Harare, 1986). Other language editions: Arabic and French.

THE VANISHING FOREST: The Human Consequences of Deforestation (Zed Books, London/New Jersey, 1986 and College Press, Harare, 1986). Other language editions: French and Serbo-Croatian.

DISAPPEARED!: Technique of Terror (Zed Books, London/New Jersey, 1986). Other language editions: French, Portuguese and Spanish.

REFUGEES: The Dynamics of Displacement (Zed Books, London/New Jersey, 1986). Other language editions: French, Japanese and Spanish.

Other reports to be published include:
    Statelessness
    Autochthonous People
    Mass Expulsions
    Disaster Management
    Displaced Persons
    Protection of Children
    The Urban Child: Perspectives and Problems
    Urban Migration
    New Man-Made Disasters

* in addition to the Commission's Final Report.

ICIHI Working Group on Humanitarian Norms and Armed Conflicts

The following members of the Independent Commission helped in the preparation of this report in their individual capacities:

Pierre Graber (Convenor)	(Switzerland)
Sadruddin Aga Khan	(Iran)
Mohammed Bedjaoui	(Algeria)
Henrik Beer	(Sweden)
Sadako Ogata	(Japan)
Willibald Pahr	(Austria)
Hassan bin Talal	(Jordan)

Editorial Committee:

Rosemary Abi-Saab
Mohamed El Kouhene
Zia Rizvi

Foreword

To alleviate suffering caused by armed violence; to limit the element of passion which is a part of conflict; in short to protect man against his own excesses: such is the ambition of international humanitarian law. As Montesquieu said, 'international law is based naturally on the principle that in times of peace, nations should do the greatest good and in times of war, the least wrong.' To guarantee this and to facilitate humanitarian action were the motivating force behind the codification of humanitarian law. The process began in 1864 when the first Geneva Convention was adopted.

The last attempt at codification led to the adoption, in 1977, of the Protocols additional to the Geneva Conventions of 1949. Having presided over the 'Diplomatic Conference on the Reaffirmation and Development of International Humanitarian Law' (1974-77) which resulted in the adoption of the protocols, I know from personal experience how difficult it has become to make progress in codification of law without compromising its effective implementation. In 1864, international humanitarian law consisted of ten articles. It now comprises six hundred, which illustrates its expansion since then as well as its richness.

In order to facilitate this progress and ensure that the law does not become dead letter, the Independent Commission felt that it was essential to highlight its significance, to explain the difficulties involved in its implementation and to reflect on the means to overcome them.

A Working Group was set up to examine humanitarian norms applicable to every kind of armed conflict. The work of this Group provided much discussion at the various plenary meetings of the Independent Commission. Finally, Judge Mohammed Bedjaoui was asked by the Group to set down the substance of those reflections.

His Report constitutes the essential part of this publication. Not every member of the Group may entirely agree with each suggestion or reflection made in it, but tribute must be paid to the high level of reflection and the aptness of expression of the author.

Judge Bedjaoui's Report accurately reflects the full range and nature of the deliberations of the Working Group. It also points to the differences with the conclusions of some of the Experts, to the extent that they value Declarations of the United Nations so much that the existing Conventions would appear to be technical appendices to them, and their application controlled by the new committees to be established by these Declarations.

It is important for me to underline in this connection that at no stage did the Independent Commission entertain the notion of substituting itself for the organisms which have traditionally dealt with questions of humanitarian law with admirable distinction and devotion. The role of the Commission is essentially a complementary one.

It is in this context that for example in 1985, we addressed a memorandum to over 110 Governments urging them to adhere to the 1977 Protocols. A number of positive replies have already been received and the members of the Commission, individually or collectively, are continuing their best endeavours to promote these instruments.

Through the publication of this volume, we hope to sensitize public opinion as well as policymakers to the need for respect of humanitarian law which, despite its shortcomings as indicated in the report, remains the best defence against arbitrary actions and violence.

Humanitarian law is a code as well as a symbol of the battle between mind and arms. As Emmanuel Mounier said, 'Law is a precarious effort to rationalize force and to move it towards love. That involves a constant struggle.'

Pierre Graber

Editorial Note

When the Independent Commission established its Working Group to examine Humanitarian Norms applicable in Armed Conflicts, its Secretariat requested a group of recognized experts to undertake research on specific aspects of humanitarian law. Their work facilitated the process of analysis and reflection of the Commission. Their contributions are annexed to the present report. We wish to record our appreciation in particular to: Georges Abi-Saab, Igor Blishchenko, Antonio Cassese, Asbjørn Eide, Konstantin Obradovic, and Jiri Toman, as well as to those who also helped in the work: Maurice Aubert, Hans-Peter Gasser, Yves Sandoz, Daniel Schindler and Michel Veuthey.

Special thanks are due to the President of the International Committee of the Red Cross, Alexandre Hay, and to its Director General, Jacques Moreillon, who shared their views during two plenary meetings of the Commission. Their statements are included in this volume.

We are grateful to Rosemary Abi-Saab who from the outset provided valuable help in the preparation of this book. We also thank Mohamed El Kouhene for his active collaboration.

Finally, we wish to thank Zed Books for its speedy publication.

Income from the sales of this book will be entirely devoted to research and dissemination of related humanitarian issues.

Pierre Graber
Convenor, Working Group on
Humanitarian Norms and
Armed Conflicts

Zia Rizvi
Secretary-General
ICIHI

Geneva, August 1986

Humanitarian law at a time of failing national and international consensus

A Report for the Independent Commission on International Humanitarian Issues

Mohammed Bedjaoui*

Contents

Introduction

---

*Judge at the International Court of Justice since 1982; Secretary-General, Algerian Council of Ministers (1962-64); Minister of Justice of Algeria (1964-70); Ambassador to France (1970-79) and to the United Nations in New York (1979-82).

1

> *'Let us dishonour War'*
> Victor Hugo

1. An old African saying reminds us that 'man alone is worse, or better, than man'. Man is capable of both good and evil; he wages war but, paradoxically, wants at the same time to subject his 'licence to kill' to a code of honour. This is precisely the concern of humanitarian law which seeks to apply a set of legal rules to humanize armed conflicts and protect the victims of situations of armed violence. But one may well ask: how is it possible to humanize what is essentially inhuman? And if human relations in war can indeed be regulated by humanitarian law, why then do we insist on drawing up a code of honour and enforcing it, instead of simply outlawing war itself?

2. Ever since man has existed, constraints of survival and subsistence have developed in him a feeling of insecurity, a fear of the future, which in turn has generated conflict. Conflict seems to be an integral part of mankind. In that sense, man is indeed 'worse than man' and 'polemology', the science of war, still has quite a future to look forward to. Conflict is not even perceived in terms of something just or unjust but as something necessary and inescapable. His heavy wings hinder man from rising above his condition.

3. That did not, however, prevent the international community from trying to discipline itself. The long process highlighted by the Briand-Kellogg Pact in 1928 was interrupted by World War II before culminating in the prohibition of war by the United Nations Charter. But polemologists are sceptical about the vain efforts of politicians and lawyers to 'police' war. To them this is like looking for a cure before knowing what the disease is, or trying to control an epidemic by writing an ode to health.[1] Thus the only thing wrong with the United Nations Charter would be to 'assume that the problem has been solved. It pretends to suppress war without knowing the actual nature, causes and rules of war. War is an absolutely general fact to be found in the oldest and most modern of all human civilizations.' In other words, as Gaston Bouthoul emphasized: 'War is not our instrument; we are the instrument of war.'[2]

4. As Hobbes wrote: 'In the state of nature, the condition of man is a condition of war of everyone against everyone.' In the 6th century B.C. Heraclitus already regarded war as 'common to all beings and the mother of all things'. Some even see war as the cause of the inequality between men and women: superiority, as Simone de Beauvoir puts it, in *The Second Sex*, is granted not to the gender which gives life but to the one which kills. Throughout the centuries war has prevailed upon hearts and minds alike. As in the poem 'Hannibal', by José Maria de Heredia, we are always hearing 'the mute stamping of marching troops' and provide war with a whole series of justifications: the divine origin of war; God rejoicing at a battle scene where soldiers are both priests and victims; war as a means of purification and regeneration; war as an essential element for the development of mankind; war as a source of progress, of virtue and of art.

5. War is regarded as inherent to social life, as an unavoidable part of some mysterious recurring cycle, 'a psychic epidemy' which contaminates mankind, a 'collective frenzy' which strikes men from time to time. It is quite like a feast, a celebration which strengthens solidarity. It is a rite involving expense, waste, destruction, sacrifice, subversion of moral principles and collective worship.

But it also has an aesthetic aspect, the flamboyant colours and lace of the warriors' finery, the delicate carvings and inlay on deadly weapons.

6. General de Gaulle, who knew war well, described thus this eternal companion of mankind: 'Arms have always been the instruments of barbarism. They relentlessly destroy order, crush hope, put prophets to death. Lucifer used them, but they were also in the Archangel's hands. They were the knave's courage, the scoundrel's honour, the slave's dignity.... They deformed, but they also shaped the world. They achieved what was best and worst, wallowing in horror or shining in glory. Theirs is a story of shame and beauty, the story of mankind.' [3]

7. Humanitarian law is beyond the controversy between polemologists and international lawyers about the inevitability of war. It has neither the ambition of polemology to explain the reasons for the permanence of conflicts, nor that of international law which declared war an unlawful act and is still trying to devise the ways and means of enforcing the ban. Humanitarian law is more pragmatic: it recognizes the existence of a violent world without attempting to explain or pacify. It is for other areas of international law and social sciences to deal with man's constant struggle to overcome the fear and insecurity which lead him to war. The basic premise of humanitarian law is a sad and daily fact of life: the existence of conflict between men. And its purpose is to limit as far as possible the effects of confrontation for all men, whether or not they have an active part in hostilities, and to alleviate suffering. Humanitarian law neither prevents men from fighting one another nor does it herald an end to war and the advent of peace; its sole aim is to regulate as closely as possible the conduct of societies during their confrontations. By doing so, it contributes to the promotion of a certain spirit of peace by intervening on the battlefields to prohibit unnecessary suffering and acts which are not dictated by military necessity. While that spirit of peace is not the actual goal of humanitarian law, it is at least an indirect consequence of it.

8. There may seem to be something elusive about such an endeavour. Albert Einstein for one had few illusions about man's capability to restrain his worst excesses. He wondered how means of destruction could generate such enthusiasm as to find men ready to sacrifice their lives. Einstein's answer was that man had within himself a thirst for hatred and destruction.[4] In *The Prince*, Machiavelli warns us against expecting too much on this score, arguing that a Prince cannot simply exercise all virtues because to preserve his position he is often forced to violate the laws of humanity, charity and religion. This was echoed a few centuries later by Clausewitz. According to him, 'War is an act of violence . . . and there are no limits to the manifestation of violence. In a situation as dangerous as war, errors of magnanimity are the worst. Indeed, moderation in the philosophy of war is absurd.'

9. Not only is the object of humanitarian law a limited one compared to the more radical aim of a complete war ban; some authors and policy-makers even consider it uncertain. Idealists intent on ridding the world of the scourge of war find it hopelessly restrictive while realists feel that humanization of violence and of the 'civilization of napalm' is decidedly utopian. Humanitarian law is constantly struggling for survival between these two extreme views, trying to avoid useless suffering if not violence itself. Humanitarian law is not utopian but a discipline based on realism: a policy of lesser evil which ultimately pays dividends since humanitarian and political concerns are not incompatible.

10. Without ever resigning himself to the inevitability of conflict, man attempts to subject war to a series of rules which set the bearable limits of the unbearable. According to the 1868 Declaration of St. Petersburg, humanitarian law should fix 'the technical limits at which the necessities of war ought to yield to the requirements of humanity'.

But is it possible to build a durable structure with such fragile materials? That is precisely the challenge facing humanitarian law. And since conflict, i.e. the use of force, continues to appear inevitable and has even rekindled the old concept of 'just war', one must ensure that it does not become a remedy which is worse than the ill that it was meant to cure: victory does not justify perverse means. A profoundly ethical dimension is therefore essential to humanitarian law for, as Albert Camus said, 'What is right must not be wronged by the very arms which are intended to defend it.'[5]

11. The Independent Commission on International Humanitarian Issues attempted to draw up a balance sheet of man's achievements, of his assets in humanizing conflicts and his liabilities in waging war. Although the efforts to humanize war are often traced back to the admirable work of Henry Dunant over a century ago, it would be wrong to believe that man never tried to 'clean up' the business of killing before that. Many nations have their own fascinating tales of chivalry and the Third World should not distrust humanitarian law because of its apparent Western flavour. Concern for the integrity and dignity of the human person is a sort of 'common heritage of mankind', not the property of one specific society.[6] It is worth emphasizing this for at least two reasons. Western public opinion, justifiably shocked by certain violations which take place in the Third World, often believes, self-righteously, that it alone can develop and observe humanitarian law. Conversely, the Third World sometimes considers the humanitarian institutions as somehow part and parcel of the developed world's strategy of domination. Humanitarian law must not become a victim of the reactions of the Third World to alien domination.

12. The Far East, the Indian subcontinent, Islamic countries, Africa and Latin America had their own principles of conduct in armed conflict. Their contribution to the establishment, development and implementation of humanitarian law must not be minimized. Neither should one ignore the horrendous examples of wanton destruction provided by the developed world for long and painful decades—colonial wars, genocide of indigenous populations, Nazi crimes during World War II, inhuman repression of those fighting for decolonization, apartheid, etc.

13. It is not the intention of the Independent Commission to embark on a technical assessment of the achievements of humanitarian institutions with the technical precision so dear to jurists, experts and technicians. Neither is it up to the Commission to list and document the examples of non-observance of humanitarian law. They exist in abundance as do the frustration and the disillusionment to which they give rise. Conversely, examples of observance of humanitarian rules do not necessarily prove the primacy of law among the protagonists whether they are States or other entities. One cannot be oblivious of the fact that compliance with humanitarian norms, while beneficial in terms of human protection, may be part of a calculated play to embarrass the enemy or simply to improve one's political image. But should we complain about such ulterior motives if their effect is to increase the number of lives that are spared? Our purpose here is first to identify the rules of the game and the actors who use them and then to assess the results in terms of observance or violation of those rules in order to suggest solutions in order to improve compliance with humanitarian rules.

14. It should therefore be noted:

(i) that while there is a kind of inflation in the number of rules, paradoxically the whole range of potential conflicts between human groups has not effectively been covered;

(ii) that the actors are more diversified and aware of their responsibilities than ever before, in the sense that the improved status of some of them can no longer justify violations of humanitarian law;

(iii) that the human, institutional and other instruments and means of control and punishment, though not lacking, are ineffective because of excessive dependence on State consent;

(iv) that conflicts have proliferated and changed in character so that humanization can no longer be ensured by adopting more and more rules of humanitarian law;

(v) that the real challenge is the proliferation of violations of humanitarian law at a time when there have never been so many rules and institutions to control them;

(vi) that at the top of the scale the threat of nuclear weapons and at the other end the increase in internal disturbances and tensions— which remain outside the field of the conventional humanitarian law—could challenge, at least in the case of the former, the scope and the very existence of humanitarian law;

(vii) and finally, that a reassessment of the meaning and purpose of humanitarian law is essential in order to face up to the nuclear challenge and to seek the best way of improving observance of humanitarian law.

15. These points can be discussed under two main headings which we shall consider in turn:

I. The law: an impressive set of rules and institutions which, paradoxically, are not without a number of serious shortcomings.

II. The facts: an increase in violations on the one hand, and the means to respond to the challenge of a world in crisis on the other.

I THE LAW

16. It is useful to attempt a simple working definition of humanitarian law: it is a set of legal rules intended to protect and aid the victims of all situations of armed violence. This rather straightforward definition is nevertheless restrictive in that it excludes situations involving refugees and disaster victims. But it is also extensive in that situations of violence cover not only actual 'armed' conflicts but internal disturbances and tensions which in fact are so far not governed by any specific legal rules.

17. An elaborate definition of humanitarian law applicable to armed conflicts has been given by the International Committee of the Red Cross (ICRC):

> 'international rules, established by treaties or custom, which are specifically intended to solve humanitarian problems directly arising from international or non-international armed conflicts and which, for humanitarian reasons, limit the right of parties to a conflict to use the methods and means of warfare of their choice or protect persons and property that are, or may be, affected by conflict.'[7]

This is the definition used here, except that we shall extend it to conflicts which are not strictly 'armed' in order to include situations of internal disturbances and tensions which although not specifically covered by international humanitarian law *stricto sensu* are nevertheless subject to rules relating to human rights. With the exclusion of refugees—whose situation is not necessarily due to an armed conflict—and disaster victims, the main feature of humanitarian law is the conflict between the need to protect the human person on the one hand and military or police requirements on the other. Operations involving the use of force have to be contained and regulated. Humanitarian law therefore has two aspects: one outlined by the law of war and the other by human rights. A distinction can, of course, be made between humanitarian law, the law of war and human rights, but they cannot be dissociated.[8]

18. Progress in the codification and development of humanitarian law has been impressive. The corpus of legal rules adopted so far includes no less than a thousand articles. There is even the theoretical possibility of an *actio popularis*, which is quite rare in international law. The four Geneva Conventions of 12 August 1949 ratified by practically all States include a common Article

1 under which States Parties not only undertake to respect the Convention but also to 'ensure respect for the Convention'. All States are in theory bound to intervene to put an end to any breach of humanitarian law wherever it may occur. A structure of remarkable density has been developed. From the normative point of view, the rules are getting more complex and codification is reaching saturation point. At the same time, huge gaps remain to be filled. There is no shortage of institutional means to protect, assist, investigate, control and sanction but since implementation is based on consensus, they are scarcely effective.

1. The normative endeavour

A. A genuine 'law of humanity'

19. The scope of the corpus of rules adopted so far is clearly impressive. Within those rules, a distinction is usually made between the codification effort undertaken in The Hague (in particular the Conventions of 1899 and 1907) and in Geneva (1864, 1929 and 1949 Conventions and 1977 Additional Protocols). In principle, the 'law of The Hague' lays down the rights and obligations of belligerents in the conduct of operations and limits the choice of the means to be used, whereas the so-called 'Geneva law' tends to protect non-fighting military personnel and persons taking no active part in hostilities. Both systems touch on a great variety of subjects. Yet, as Jean Pictet pointed out, humanitarian law is 'a law concluded by States and implemented by States'. It cannot be said that humanitarian law is utopian. It provides an intricate network of rules involving specific legal obligations for States. As Judge Max Huber put it: 'From a strictly legal point of view, a genuine law of humanity has been created whereby the human person, human integrity and human dignity are protected in the name of a moral principle towering far above the boundaries of international law and politics.'

20. Traditional law as codified or developed by the Geneva Conference of 1864, the Brussels Conference of 1874 and the Hague Conferences of 1899 and 1907 only regulated armed conflicts between States and neutrality. It did not extend to civil wars or, at a lower level, to internal disturbances and tensions. In that traditional framework, war on land and on the sea (air warfare scarcely existed at the time), categories of legitimate combatants, means of combat, weapons, methods of warfare, and protection of war victims (injured, sick and shipwrecked) were regulated in some detail.

21. There were new developments connected with modern armed conflicts:

- New categories of combatants: partisans during World War II and 'guerrillas' in national liberation struggles.
- New means of destruction and warfare: fighter planes, chemical, bacteriological and nuclear weapons.
- Finally, the complexity of civil wars and the new categories and sub-categories of conflicts: non-international armed conflicts distinct from both national liberation struggles—recognized as international conflicts—and situations of internal disturbances and tensions which have yet to be covered by the conventional humanitarian law.

22. Legitimate combatants now include not only members of the regular armed forces but, under certain conditions, militiamen, volunteer corps, organized resistance fighters and guerrillas. Mercenaries, however, are excluded from the status of combatant or prisoner of war. The means of combat have also given rise to new rules: apart from poison and toxic weapons, dum dum bullets, explosive projectiles under 400 grammes and asphyxiating gases, which were all banned by the law of The Hague, and chemical and bacteriological weapons, which were prohibited by the 1925 Geneva Protocol, 'fragment weapons', mines, booby traps and incendiary devices were banned by a 1980 Convention.

23. In short, the conduct of military operations follows a set of rules because 'The rights of belligerents to adopt means of injuring the enemy is not unlimited' (as already stated by Article 22 of the 1907 Convention relating to the laws and customs of war on land). At present, those general rules govern a variety of issues such as the weapons used, the status of combatants, the status of medical personnel and facilities, the protection of the cultural heritage, the protection of journalists on perilous missions, etc. Forbidden weapons are those which cause unnecessary suffering to non-fighting persons or make their death inevitable. The Regulations relating to the laws and customs of war on land contained in the Fourth Hague Convention of 1907 prohibited the use of 'arms, projectiles, or material calculated to cause unnecessary suffering' (Article 23). Those Regulations merely reasserted the 1868

St. Petersburg Declaration and the Hague Declaration of 1899.
24. A superficial reading of the texts which constitute the actual substance of humanitarian law—such as the above-mentioned Declarations, the work of the 1907 Peace Conference, the Geneva Protocol of 17 June 1925, the Geneva Conventions of 1929 and 1949 and the Additional Protocols of 1977—reveals two main underlying principles. The first is the distinction between combatants (theoretically the only persons affected by the conflict) and the non-combatants (who should be spared). The second is the obligation not to cause unnecessary harm to combatants. It is with these two general and essential principles in mind that humanitarian law, at a very early stage, prohibited certain types of weapons either because of their indiscriminate effect on combatants and civilians or because of the unnecessary harm caused to combatants.
25. Undoubtedly because a great many rules of humanitarian law are so fundamental to the respect of the human person and 'elementary considerations of humanity' (those were the terms used by the International Court of Justice in its 1949 Judgement in the Corfu Channel Case), accession to the Hague and Geneva Conventions has been practically universal. The fundamental rules are or should be observed by all States not only because they have undertaken to do so by ratifying those Conventions but because those rules have become intransgressible principles of international customary law. 'In view of their impartial character and the higher values for which they stand, and also because of their long historical tradition and their extension throughout the world, we may now assert that the Geneva and Hague Conventions, to a great extent, are no longer merely reciprocal treaties, limited to the framework of relations between states, but have become absolute and universal commitments.'[9]
26. The Nuremberg International Military Tribunal had already found that the humanitarian rules included in the 1907 Hague Convention and the 1929 Geneva Convention were so firmly entrenched in human consciousness as to be considered part of general international law.[10] These 'Great Charters of Humanity', the 1907 and 1929 Conventions, to which should be added the almost universally ratified Geneva Conventions of 1949, are peremptory norms: they are intransgressible and binding even for the handful of non-ratifying States. The 1969 Vienna Convention on the Law of Treaties of 25 May 1969 defines in Article 53 what is meant by

a 'peremptory norm of international law' (*jus cogens*) giving as an example of such norms in Article 60 'provisions relating to the protection of the human person contained in treaties of a humanitarian character'.

27. It can be seen that the humanitarian Conventions recognize the right for States to denounce the instrument. But instead of providing Parties with a loophole this has proved to be a source of strength. The fact that no Power has ever made use of its right to denounce one of these Conventions shows that no State feels able to reject such basic rules of civilization.

28. The extensive codification of humanitarian law, universal accession and the non-use and obsolescence of the denunciation clause have thus provided the international community with a corpus of treaty rules most of which have become customary and which reflect the most universally recognized humanitarian principles. These rules indicate the normal conduct and behaviour expected of States.

29. This set of rules is not perfect, however. One difficulty is the sheer intricacy and complexity of the regulations, which is, as it were, the price to pay for the extensive codification of humanitarian law. As for the reasons for the present violations of humanitarian law, it will appear that one of them is precisely the complexity of a number of rules which makes them difficult to implement.

30. A distinction has traditionally been made between the so-called law of The Hague (chiefly the Hague Conventions of 1899 and 1907 governing primarily the conduct of military operations) and the so-called law of Geneva (Geneva Conventions protecting persons *hors de combat* and not taking part in the hostilities). The distinction is now rather obsolete especially since one of the achievements of the 1977 Protocols has been to integrate both components of humanitarian law, essentially to ensure better protection of civilians. The Protocols reasserted and updated the principles governing the conduct of hostilities taking into account the changes in methods and means of combat. These principles are laid down not only in Protocol I, but also in Protocol II.

A number of gaps and shortcomings remain, however, and should be dealt with in the light of technological progress. That is the case *inter alia* concerning neutrality and the improvement of marking and identifying techniques for medical transport.

31. It would seem unrealistic to expect in the near future any further codification and development of humanitarian law, just as it is unlikely that 'a little more law', i.e. further progress in codification, might prove the right kind of remedy to stem the tide of present-day violations of humanitarian law. The present state of international relations is not really conducive to further codification efforts.

Despite the possible feeling of saturation regarding the present state of codification, a great deal remains to be done to humanize the whole field of human conflict. Paradoxically, there are still many gaps and deficiencies in the present system.

B. The 'law of humanity' and its deficiency vis-à-vis a 'nuclear holocaust'

32. Some of the gaps and deficiencies of humanitarian law are such that, in qualitative terms, they seriously undermine its scope and credibility.

33. At the top end of the scale is the failure to deal with the 'nuclear issue' in international armed conflicts. To clarify the matter it should be recalled that, important though they may be, the aims of humanitarian law are extremely modest. Humanitarian law does not prohibit war; that is the concern of another part of international law which deprives States of their traditional power to wage war except for the 'inherent' right of self-defence enshrined in Article 51 of the United Nations Charter. Humanitarian law applies at a later stage, i.e. when conflict has already started (by aggression, military intervention, self-defence, etc); it does not attempt to condemn or justify, merely to 'control' and 'humanize' the conflict. To achieve this, it can rely on a set of various rules and on two main principles, namely the crucial distinction between combatants and non-combatants and the obligation to avoid causing 'unnecessary harm' to combatants.

34. The fundamental texts mentioned above such as the St. Petersburg Declaration of 1868, the Hague Declaration of 1899 and 1907, the Geneva Protocol of 1925, the Geneva Conventions of 1864, 1929 and 1949 and the Additional Protocols of 1977 all emphasize the prohibition of arms and means of combat which victimize indiscriminately or cause unnecessary suffering to combatants. But what about nuclear weapons? First of all it might be useful to recall the definition of the 1954 Protocols to the Brussels

Treaty of Collaboration and Collective Self-Defence among Western European States:

> An atomic weapon is defined as any weapon which contains, or is designed to contain or utilize, nuclear fuel or radioactive isotopes and which, by explosion or other uncontrolled nuclear transformation of the nuclear fuel, or by radioactivity of the nuclear fuel or radioactive isotopes, is capable of mass destruction, mass injury or mass poisoning.

Speaking of napalm, the ICRC[11] observed that by its very nature it caused unnecessary suffering and on account of its indiscriminate character it harmed civilian populations and combatants alike. Its consequences escape the control of those employing it. This reasoning applies equally to the nuclear arms.

35. In the present state of scientific development at least, nuclear weapons can be expected to cause indiscriminate victims among combatants and non-combatants alike, as well as unnecessary suffering among both categories. The very nature of this blind weapon therefore has a destabilizing effect on humanitarian law which regulates discernment of the type of weapon used. Nuclear weapons, the ultimate evil, destabilize humanitarian law which is the law of the lesser evil. *The existence of nuclear weapons is therefore a challenge to the very existence of humanitarian law*. Until scientists are able to develop a 'clean' nuclear weapon which would distinguish between combatants and non-combatants, nuclear weapons will clearly have indiscriminate effects and constitute an absolute challenge to humanitarian law. *Atomic warfare and humanitarian law therefore appear to be mutually exclusive*: the existence of the one automatically implies the non-existence of the other. Instead of a clean nuclear weapon with controllable and discriminate effects, scientists have developed the so-called neutron bomb, the ultimate denial of humanitarian law which kills living beings while causing minimal material destruction.

36. It should be noted that this whole analysis is based on the fact that humanitarian law does not prohibit any given weapon *per se*. It only prohibits weapons in so far as they go beyond the object of destroying the enemy and kill civilian populations or cause unnecessary suffering to enemy forces. Indeed humanitarian law only bans weapons in so far as they have indiscriminate effects. Its basic principles do not provide sufficient grounds for prohibiting hypothetical nuclear weapons which would not have such effects and would therefore be used only against military objectives (persons or property).

37. It is probably with this in mind that some authors make the distinction—for the purpose of humanitarian law—between strategic and tactical nuclear weapons. Although approaching the subject with some caution, Professor Roger Pinto considers that 'a rule can apparently be inferred from the attitude of nuclear powers prohibiting the use of strategic weapons on a reciprocal basis'. He quite rightly adds that: 'The principles of the law of armed conflict governing the use of weapons of mass and uncontrolled destruction necessarily imply the protection of non-combatants and future generations, and the prohibition of strategic weapons.'[12]As for tactical weapons, their use would be authorized in as much as they would not belong to the category of weapons of mass destruction, even though their effects may be greater than the bombs which destroyed Hiroshima and Nagasaki.

38. In fact all the conceptual efforts made to draw a distinction between nuclear weapons to justify the use of some of them have failed. Because of their very nature nuclear weapons cannot be the subject of such fine distinctions. Moreover tactical nuclear weapons can still cause as much or even more radiation than the Hiroshima or Nagasaki bombs. It is also likely that the use of such weapons would lead to retaliation and ultimately to total nuclear war. The limited use of nuclear weapons assumes that the enemy will also respond with the same type of small weapons, not allowing for the fact that rationality will decline or even disappear once the fatal initial move has sparked off the conflict.

39. Although the principle of respect for non-combatants and civilians had been proclaimed as the primary rule of humanitarian law, civilians have been the main victims of major conflicts with, as an aggravating circumstance in World War II, the nuclear annihilation of cities. The Promethean emergence of nuclear weapons among the means of destruction openly flouted the universal rule of protection of civilian populations. Inevitably therefore, there were considerable misgivings when the International Nuremberg Military Tribunal included among the list of war crimes the wanton destruction of towns and villages. Indeed, a few months earlier the allied armed forces had themselves destroyed several German cities and used nuclear weapons to wipe out the innocent civilians of Hiroshima and Nagasaki. That is probably the reason

15

why the Nuremberg Tribunal did not indict anyone for the destruction of towns and villages. The nuclear debate was already looming at that very early stage.

40. It became far more acute at the Diplomatic Conference which drafted the four Geneva Conventions of 12 August 1949. Proposals to prohibit the use of nuclear weapons were duly submitted, but the Conference with some unease decided that it did not have the authority to deal with the issue. The latent contradiction was all the more apparent as the Conference could not fail to reassert and develop the principle of respect for civilian populations. In 1956, when the ICRC opened the nuclear debate at the International Conference of the Red Cross in New Delhi, the issue was sidestepped yet again.

The unavoidable contradiction re-emerged at the Diplomatic Conference which adopted the 1977 Protocols updating the 1949 Conventions. A number of participating nuclear powers made a point of formally excluding any discussion of nuclear weapons. The United Kingdom and the United States formally confirmed their position by making reservations when signing the Protocol. France stated for the record during the final meetings that it regarded nuclear weapons as outside the scope of Protocol I. Moreover, during the general debate, Sweden requested that the Conference should consider only the problems arising out of classical warfare, leaving aside nuclear as well as bacteriological and chemical weapons. On the other hand, when Article 35 of Protocol I on 'Fundamental Rules' was adopted by consensus, India declared it had joined in the consensus because the rules of that Article covered in its view all types of weapons, including nuclear weapons.

41. From the legal point of view, there was therefore a certain amount of confusion at least at first glance. While these contrasting statements did not prompt any specific positive or negative response by other participating States, this does not amount to tacit approval of their content since they were in fact contradictory, and some were made after the meetings. Besides, there can be no such thing as tacit approval in such a vital matter. But, above all, the declarations of a handful of States obviously cannot be invoked against a general principle established by earlier Conventions which had meanwhile become part of international customary law.

42. It should further be noted that when an ad hoc Committee was set up by the Conference to draw up a list of 'conventional' weapons liable to cause unnecessary harm, the issue of nuclear weapons as non-conventional weapons re-emerged and was evaded yet again.

From the above considerations, it is therefore clear:

(i) that nuclear Powers would not discuss the regulation or possible limitation, by humanitarian law, of the use of nuclear weapons;

(ii) that there was no substantive debate on the nuclear issue at the 1974-1977 Conference and that no specific solution was put forward;

(iii) that it would be wrong, however, to infer that the use of nuclear weapons is lawful since Protocol I in no way annulled the general customary rules applicable to all methods and means of combat;

(iv) that nuclear weapons were not specifically outside the scope of Protocol I since the Protocol reasserted and endorsed those peremptory customary rules;

(v) that the opposite would be quite absurd since it would amount to prohibiting unnecessary suffering only when inflicted by conventional but not by nuclear weapons;

(vi) finally, that Protocol I if anything gave new impetus to the debate on the prohibition of nuclear weapons.

43. The present legal status of nuclear weapons therefore remains unsatisfactory. The problem of the unlawfulness of that means of combat is the same as it was before Protocol I. There is no specific international Convention on the unlawfulness of nuclear weapons and it would be wrong to believe that such a Convention could be negotiated in the present circumstances, or that it could resolve the nuclear dilemma even if it appears in the interest of States to engage in negotiations on an issue involving grave uncertainty for the scope and the very existence of humanitarian law.

44. Humanitarian law continues to prohibit the use of weapons with indiscriminate effects liable to cause unnecessary suffering and therefore cannot be regarded as authorizing the use of nuclear weapons which are incapable of avoiding such effects. The interpretation by analogy of a number of humanitarian conventions and even of *jus cogens* implies a ban on nuclear weapons. Exposure to radiation can and should be assimilated to exposure to poisonous, harmful or deadly substances prohibited by the Hague Regulations of 1899 and 1907. And even if interpretation by analogy were ruled out, to allow the lawful use of nuclear weapons would give rise to an absurd and untenable situation since it would mean that the prohibition of the use of asphyxiating gases on the basis of the 1925 Geneva Protocol cannot be extended to far more harmful nuclear clouds.

45. Moreover the so-called Martens clause in the Hague Convention of 1907 anticipating the rapid development of military technology stipulates that for cases not governed by existing rules (which could refer to the 'nuclear issue'), human persons remain under the protection of the principles of humanity and in particular 'under the protection and the rule of the principles of the law of nations, as they result from the usages established among civilized peoples, from the laws of humanity and the dictates of the public conscience'. Finally a number of United Nations General Assembly resolutions condemn the use of nuclear weapons as inconsistent with the United Nations Charter and humanitarian law and as a crime against humanity and civilization. Even though General Assembly resolutions are not binding, they reformulate general principles of humanitarian law which in turn are binding as the expression of international customary law.

C. A 'law of humanity' excluded in situations of internal disturbances and tensions

46. International law prohibits the use of force in international relations and the United Nations Charter spelled out that prohibition, which has become a customary rule, in Article 2, paragraph 4. In municipal law, a different situation prevails in as much as the State forbids the use of force by everyone but itself. In other words, the State enjoys the discretionary power to intervene with its troops, police forces, etc, to prevent or suppress internal disturbances and tensions.

47. There is no doubt that humanitarian law has made considerable progress. Before the four Geneva Conventions of 12 August 1949 it could protect only the victims of wars between States. After 1949, under Article 3 which is the same in all four Conventions, humanitarian law applies also to non-international conflicts. The 1977 Protocols went one step further to improve the implementation of humanitarian law within State boundaries. Protocol I grants minimum guarantees to any person affected by the conflict who does not enjoy a more favourable protective status under the 1949

Conventions and the Protocols (Article 75). That protection is meant for all those who were not protected or insufficiently protected before 1977, in particular the nationals of a Party to the conflict. The individual is now protected not only against the enemy, but against his own government which is a step towards universal protection of the victims of armed conflicts.

These minimum guarantees are also to be found in Protocol II. They supplement the embryonic protection provided by common Article 3 of the 1949 Conventions. But the effective implementation of these guarantees, however minimal, is still subject to a major prerequisite: the existence of an armed conflict within the meaning of the Protocols. By specifying the concept of non-international armed conflicts, Protocol II limited its scope to conflicts of a given intensity. It does not extend to situations of internal disturbances and tensions which do not reach that threshold. But today these are precisely the most frequent and prevalent situations.

48. Specialists refer to 'internal disturbances' when, in the absence of an 'armed conflict', the State uses force to maintain or re-establish law and order and the rule of law, and to 'internal tensions' when in the absence of 'internal disturbances' it resorts to the preventive use of force to preserve peace and the rule of law. Although there is no 'armed conflict', the seriousness and duration of the situation leads the State to use force. It is only too well known how often the use of force leads to mass arrests, disappearances, summary executions, suspension of fundamental legal rights, terrorist acts, taking of hostages, torture, etc.

A balance is hardly ever struck between the requirements of law and order and the observance of humanitarian law. It is therefore very desirable during such disturbances and tensions to humanize the confrontation between the State and individuals or groups of individuals to avoid any arbitrary conduct on either side. It is certainly not easy to distinguish between disturbances and tensions, and indeed between internal disturbances and non-international armed conflicts. When does a situation cease to pertain to the maintenance of law and order and become an armed conflict? Who is going to decide when the threshold is crossed, making Protocol II applicable? While human rights do apply in situations of internal disturbances and tensions, this is not enough, especially as they are often restricted by the proclamation of a state of emergency. Moreover human rights are less suited to situations of armed violence than humanitarian law.

49. In its present state, humanitarian law does not provide a sound legal basis for the ICRC to intervene in such situations, frequent though they may be, involving all kinds of racial riots, violent strikes and social tensions. In these situations it is not two sovereign international entities who are fighting, but a sovereign State and its own subjects, which raises the delicate question of interference in the internal affairs of States by a foreign body. One of the fundamental State attributes is the maintenance of law and order. This is regarded by the State as its own prerogative to be shared with no one else, which raises another delicate problem, i.e. the lawfulness of a foreign 'control' that could be exercised by the ICRC. On the other hand, clearly some kind of humanitarian protection is needed in these situations of disturbances and tensions since the classical and usual spiral of violence and repression inevitably leads to situations where the individual is no longer protected by the State, either because the State is no longer able to maintain law and order or because it is itself violating humanitarian norms or the essential principles of human rights.

50. So far, the ICRC has exercised what is known as '*ad hoc* protection' under Article VI, paragraph 5 of the Statutes of the International Red Cross which provides that the ICRC is a 'neutral institution whose humanitarian work is carried out particularly in time of war, civil war, or internal strife . . .'. This kind of protection can also be derived *inter alia* from Resolution VI of the 24th International Conference of the Red Cross (Manila 1981), which, after considering that 'the International Committee of the Red Cross is not always able to discharge its humanitarian activities in internal disturbances and tensions', makes 'a solemn appeal that the rules of international humanitarian law and the universally recognized humanitarian principles be safeguarded at all times and in all circumstances and that the International Committee of the Red Cross be granted all the facilities necessary to discharge the humanitarian mandate confided to it by the international community'.

Finally the ICRC can rely on its traditional role as an initiator under Article IV of its Statutes, which defines it 'as a neutral institution, especially in case of . . . internal strife'.

The grounds for intervening, however, remain fragile in that the State concerned does not have to accept *ad hoc* ICRC action. The

International Committee has nevertheless made some 2,000 visits in over 90 countries, covering half a million prisoners, because it has been persuasive enough to present its action as beneficial not only to the detainees but also to the State concerned.

51. Ultimately, the gaps in humanitarian law are to be found at both ends of the spectrum: at the top end is the nuclear questions, and at the lower end the legal vacuum concerning situations of internal disturbances and tensions. These gaps reduce the scope of humanitarian law, undermine its effectiveness or, in the case of nuclear weapons, challenge its very existence. The insufficient means of control and sanctions only make matters worse.

2. The institutional endeavour: diverse means, elusive results

52. The stumbling block of all humanitarian law is the issue of control and punishment. The legal basis and the institutions are there. The responsibility of States Parties is clearly laid down in the main instruments of humanitarian law. Mechanisms such as the 'Protecting Power' and 'substitutes' provide the theroretical means to ensure observance of humanitarian law, in particular where prisoners of war are concerned. The role of the ICRC concerning control is both effective and efficient. The role of the United Nations, mentioned in Article 89 of Protocol I, can also be considerable if that provision is actually implemented. Finally the International Fact Finding Commission to be set up under Article 90 of Protocol I could ensure control and punishment if it is ever set up. But as we shall see the whole system of control remains subservient to the will of States. The establishment and of course the actual operation of these mechanisms is ultimately subject to State consent.

A. Control

53. Each Contracting Party naturally enjoys, within the framework of the humanitarian conventions in force, the right to control compliance with the commitments entered into by the other Parties as well as the obligation to put an end to the violations committed by its own forces. Moreoever the Geneva Conventions of 12 August 1949 established the 'Protecting Power' i.e. a State designated by another State to protect its interests and those of its nationals vis-à-vis a third State.

The Protecting Power's role is essentially to protect prisoners of war and civilian internees. However the mechanism has hardly ever been used for a variety of reasons including the difficulty of finding a neutral State acceptable to both belligerent States which would be able and willing to undertake this task. This is probably why the Geneva Conventions of 1949 also provided for substitutes for Protecting Powers. But this system proved rather cumbersome. At times the ICRC has assumed *de facto* the role of 'subsitute' or 'quasi-substitute'—although in such cases it might then become rather difficult to define its acts from a legal point of view.

B. Sanctions

54. As mentioned above, Parties to the 1949 Geneva Conventions are under the obligation to put an end to violations of humanitarian law. They also have the authority to punish grave violations regarded as war crimes which are imprescriptible and punishable anywhere. The 1949 Conventions also include an international enquiry procedure which has never yet been used because of its dependence on an agreement between the Parties. But Protocol I of 1977 provided for a Fact-Finding Commission to investigate any alleged violation of humanitarian law even without the consent of the Party against which the allegations are made, and which consists of fifteen members 'of high moral standing and acknowledged impartiality' elected for five years by the Contracting Parties which have recognized the competence of the Commission. The Commission has yet to come into operation and so far there are still no practical means of ensuring impartial fact-finding and of applying possible sanctions as a result.

55. Article 89 of Protocol I provides that 'In situations of serious violations of the Conventions or of this Protocol, the High Contracting Parties undertake to act, jointly or individually, in co-operation with the United Nations and in conformity with the United Nations Charter'. As we already pointed out earlier on, a theoretical *actio popularis* exists under common Article 1 of the four 1949 Conventions which provides that 'The High Contracting Parties undertake to respect and to ensure respect for the present Convention in all circumstances'. Even if this Article were only to apply within the State to ensure observance of humanitarian rules and punish those responsible which are under its jurisdiction, the provisions of Article 89 would still present interesting prospects for individual or joint State action with the co-operation of the United Nations.

56. It should also be noted that breaches of humanitarian law can give rise to a sanction by an international judicial body. Thus in 1984, Nicaragua filed before the International Court of Justice an application against the United States of America which it accused of undertaking military and paramilitary action in Nicaragua and against it and in particular of helping counter-revolutionary forces (known as *contras*) which are opposed to the government in power in Managua. On 27 June 1986, the International Court of Justice gave its judgement in which, without pronouncing on the atrocities committed by the *contras* themselves, it recognized *inter alia* the responsibility of the United States Government for producing and distributing among the *contras* a manual on psychological warfare inciting violations of humanitarian law which had been used by United States agents to train *contra* forces.

57. In short the international community today can rely on a humanitarian law applicable in international and non-international armed conflicts and which can potentially be extended to situations of internal disturbances and tensions and to nuclear war. It can also rely on enforcement mechanisms. But the obstacles which prevent implementation have proliferated. The worsening international climate has increased the tendency to resort to the use of force. As Alexandre Hay, President of ICRC, bitterly remarked: 'Humanitarian concerns have to settle for a second place'. A closer look should be taken at this tendency and at the possible means of reversing the trend.

II—THE FACTS

1. Violations of humanitarian law and their causes

A. The painful truth

58. First of all, one has to be sure whether, in fact, there are more and more violations of humanitarian law all over the world. Any pessimistic bias or optical illusions must be avoided. The progress in communications has turned the world into one big village where everyone knows what is going on everywhere else and this could give the distorted impression that a crisis has developed, when in fact the violations of humanitarian law are neither worse nor more frequent than before. A careful assessment is therefore essential.

(a) Proliferation of 'local' wars

59. The history of humanity is one long succession of wars and conflicts. It is the strange destiny of mankind that crime does pay and in certain respects is the catalyst of history or, as the Chinese saying goes: 'he who steals a cow is a thief, he who robs a nation is a prince'. In over 3,400 years of documented human history, only 250 have been years of peace. War is thus the normal state of relations between men.

60. But something new has emerged during the last decades. World peace has indeed been preserved for the past forty years and a Third World War has been avoided so far. This would seem quite an achievement in an age more dangerous than that of the League of Nations, because of nuclear weapons. But the statement should be qualified because of the considerable number of local wars which have broken out since 1945. Often under the umbrella of mutual nuclear deterrence, war has proliferated with a limited number of participants and means of warfare and within specific boundaries. Approximately 150 wars or conflicts have been fought since the end of World War II claiming some 20 million lives. Polemological institutes have counted a mere 26 days of total peace since the end of World War II. That of course depends on what is meant by a day without war. But even with less strict criteria, other calculations find an average of three warless days per year since 1945, which is hardly more encouraging news. In other words, at the present time, for 362 days out of 365, there is an active conflict going on somewhere in the world.

(b) Proliferation of internal conflicts

61. It should also be noted that apart from these 'local wars' between States, there are a number of 'internal conflicts', partly an illustration of the weakness and precariousness of newly independent States faced with the problems of underdevelopment and a host of political contradictions and socio-economic difficulties. Only by eliminating their causes can there be less use of force and better observance of humanitarian law.

(c) *Increasing violations of humanitarian law*

62. For a decade or two, conflicts have clearly been more frequent, more serious, and more radicalized. The Iran-Iraq war has been going on longer than World War II. Prisoners of war in conflicts like the Ogaden or Western Sahara have been held for over twice the period of detention of World War II prisoners. The fate of refugees in the camps on the Thai-Kampuchean border reminds us more and more of the situation in Palestinian camps, dragging on and on for years, with no solution in sight.

Many more examples could be given. Situations are becoming more complex, ideologies more extreme and crises have a greater tendency to culminate in war.

63. The increasing violations of humanitarian law are well illustrated by the casualty distribution in recent conflicts. During World War I, 95% of casualties were combatants and only 5% civilian. World War II saw a complete reversal of the picture with 75% civilian and 25% combatant casualties. In some contemporary wars, over 90% of casualties are civilians. A Third World War ending in a nuclear holocaust would ensure a 100% civilian casualty rate. The use of weapons of mass destruction can only lead to the assertion of the 'total war' concept which is by definition a negation of humanitarian law and of all forms of life.

B. External causes of violations

(a) 'Total war'

64. The increasing number of violations of humanitarian law is partly due to political causes. The obstacles to the observance of law can be inherent in the causes of conflict because violence and excesses are inherent in any conflict situation. 'Total war' is an alarming novelty in the already tormented world landscape. It involves mobilizing all possible means to achieve ends which are not always clearly defined or merely to avenge earlier defeats. It also involves the indiscriminate use of violence and the worst possible atrocities against civilians, the wanton destruction of property, and pursuit of hostilities beyond unconditional surrender, even up to the total annihilation of the enemy. Contemporary technological progress has considerably increased the means of waging this type of warfare.

(b) '... and evermore blood feeds the sun'

65. We are no longer in the pre-Columbian time when religious beliefs called for war. The 'flowered treaty' required that blood be fed to the sun, thus making war a blood tribute to be paid for life or survival. Although present-day beliefs have evolved, one may well wonder whether mentalities have changed as much. Has man in fact left the paleolithic age, the pre-Columbian era or the crusades behind him? For Clausewitz, war has remained a means to pursue a political end. Economists and polemologists tell us that war, the blood tribute paid to the pre-Columbian sun is also the blood tribute paid to the god of economic growth in contemporary societies which are prisoners of their own industrial and military complexes. People believe that they die for their country or for an ideal. In fact they often die for arms-traders.

(c) A chain reaction

66. We live in a time of violence, of erosion of family structure, of centrifugal forces at the national level, of acute conflict in labour relations. Our traditional beliefs are shadowed by doubts. General anxiety has become the lot of man in the face of scientific, technological and even medical progress. Ethical barriers have broken down, fundamental moral values are questioned and man is engulfed by waves of fear and insecurity. In our own conscience, in the family, at school, at work, in the community, in the country and finally in international relations, negative forces are at work. The national consensus is being eroded and the international consensus seriously undermined.

67. The erosion is visible at every level. The proliferation of authoritarian regimes or the quest for charismatic leaders are a reflection of our fear and uncertainty. Fear pervades human society. This is why people look for 'the strong man whom providence would send to dissipate human anxieties'. The contemporary world seems fascinated by the totalitarian model which deifies those in power. Governments rule and citizens obey: such is the individual and collective reflex today.

(d) The two challenges

68. There are two challenges to face. The first is how gradually to reduce intolerance and find a common denominator even with extremists who are inspired by leaders who reject the universality of man because their 'truth' is so absolute that it leaves no room for any other. This is what characterizes contemporary society. But this is not something new. The world has already had such experiences, for instance at the time of the wars of religion. From that point of view, no one has any lessons to give to others, neither for the recent nor more distant past. Terrorism is one of the features of this type of extremism.

69. The second challenge is to learn to live in a certain state of chaos. If legal norms are increasingly flouted, it may be partly because of the proliferation of unclear texts but even more because of a different perception of law in different parts of the world. Of course the observance of texts is more important than it ever has been. But it has become clear that observance of legal norms is no longer what it used to be. The established order may at times appear unjust to some. Consequently the mere thought of observing the legal norms which uphold that order seems unacceptable to them.

Moreover the structure of power has changed in many countries. It is not always known who is in control in some States and who is the right interlocutor to contact to get something done. To survive in such a chaotic environment it is all the more essential to safeguard a set of fundamental principles and to look for the deeper and more durable common features in mankind.

(e) The alarming and general decline of law[13]

70. The present worsening situation inevitably involves loss of respect for the rule of law in general and for the rules of humanitarian law in particular. In this connection, the ICRC aptly stated:

> This tendency appears to correspond to a fairly general decline in respect for the rule of law, internally and internationally. At the national level, the power structures—all too often harassed by an unsteady economic situation or by ethnic, ideological or other tensions—become more rigid or on the contrary break up in chaos; both situations lead to arbitrary action and violence against defenceless victims.'[14]

C. The causes of violations specific to humanitarian law

(a) Excessive dependence on State consent

71. As mentioned earlier on, humanitarian law, a law of States concluded by States, is heavily dependent on the will of States. Yet the most fundamental rules of humanitarian law initially laid down in treaties by the States themselves should no longer be dependent on their consent as they have become universal customary rules gradually accepted by mankind as a whole. In its recent Judgement of 27 June 1986 in the case concerning *Military and paramilitary activities in and against Nicaragua (Nicaragua v. United States of America)*, the International Court of Justice stressed the customary character of a number of fundamental rules of the Geneva Conventions of 12 August 1949. The indisputable fact remains however that in some fields, in particular as regards implementating mechanisms and therefore institutional and procedural matters, the enforcement of that customary law is still largely dependent on the consent and political will of States.

(b) Rules without immediate visibility

72. One of the reasons for non-enforcement or incomplete observance of humanitarian law lies in the increasing complexity of some of its norms. The rules are at times difficult to grasp and not always completely clear, especially in times of crisis and in combat situations. There is no doubt that humanitarian law needs to be rendered more easily accessible to those who, without special legal training, are required to follow it.

(c) An increasing number of actors

73. Today, a great number of people are involved in implementing humanitarian law. Among the situational or inherent obstacles to observance, there is the sheer number of rules involved. The inclusion of new actors, such as resistance fighters, partisans and more recently guerrilla fighters, as legitimate combatants (with their rights and obligations) should have led to greater observance since these new actors have been granted new responsibilities. But with technical progress on the one hand and the new forms of warfare on the other—in particular the advent of total war—actors have continued to proliferate. Despite its qualitative improvements, humanitarian law is not close enough to the real world. This is particularly the case for the crucial distinction between civilians and combatants. Reality has become more complex and distinctions more uncertain. Total conflicts with total mobilization of

human and economic resources have meant an increasing participation of civilian facilities and of civilians themselves in the war
efforts, thus blurring the distinction between civilians and combatants, especially for those responsible for applying humanitarian
law.

74. These are some of the causes of non-observance of humanitarian norms. But is there a way to improve the situation? The main
one, indeed the radical remedy, would of course be an improvement in the international political climate and the patient and loyal
quest on all sides for a new consensus based on greater equity and
justice. The violence of a few desperados would then become irrele-
vant. This ideal theoretical solution goes beyond the scope of the
present study on humanitarian law. But is there anything else within
the framework of humanitarian law or in its immediate vicinity
that could help? One answer would be for more States to ratify
the 1977 Geneva Protocols.

2. The need to ratify the 1977 Protocols

75. Better observance of humanitarian law will certainly not be
achieved through further efforts of codification and progressive
development of law. It would be wrong to believe that a 'few more
rules', a 'little more law' might do the trick. Indeed we already
have the rules and the law. What we need is to find means of
implementation. It may therefore seem somewhat illogical to stress
this objective on the one hand and encourage States to ratify the
1977 Protocols on the other, thereby extending humanitarian law
even further. Obviously, some clarification is needed.

76. The two Protocols of 17 June 1977 do not actually constitute
a set of new legal rules. Indeed the Protocols merely give a new
emphasis to the existing law and to the corpus of humanitarian rules
laid down in the Geneva Conventions of 12 August 1949. Their
aim therefore is to safeguard what has already been achieved. But
as law is never static, it also has to be adapted, improved, made
easier to apply. This is precisely what the Additional Protocols are
meant to do. They do not transform, they merely update the four
Geneva Conventions of 1949. Their main purpose is to emphasize
the fact that 'military requirements' have to be carefully defined
to prevent States from taking advantage of them.

77. It is useful to recall the actual contents of the two Protocols.

Protocol I dealing with international armed conflicts updates the means and methods of combat and ensures better protection of civilian populations by prohibiting attacks which have indiscriminate effects. By considering wars of national liberation as international armed conflicts, it also reassesses the concept of combatant and extends it to guerrillas who are recognized as legitimate combatants and thus eligible for prisoner-of-war status. That status is not, however, granted to mercenaries. Regarding the indiscriminate effects of weapons and the choice of weapons, the shadow of a ban on nuclear weapons is of course distinguishable behind Protocol I which is why, with the exception of China, the nuclear powers are reticent to ratify it. In reality, Protocol I does not add anything new to what was stated in the 1949 Geneva Conventions. It did not renew the nuclear debate but merely brought the subject up again on practically the same basis as when nuclear weapons first appeared. There are certainly no grounds for refusing to ratify Protocol I for this reason alone, since the Geneva Conventions of 1949 have already been ratified.

78. Protocol II for its part concerns non-international armed conflicts i.e. internal confrontations of high intensity which fall within the category of armed conflicts. Situations of a lower intensity such as cases of internal disturbances and tensions are explicitly excluded by Protocol II. In fact the only change in Protocol II compared to common Article 3 of the 1949 Geneva Conventions (on the subject of non-international armed conflicts) is an improvement in the protection of civilian populations and detainees, as well as the protection of medical stations and health personnel.

79. Nevertheless, the two Additional Protocols adopted by the Diplomatic Conference on 8 June 1977 (which entered into force on 8 December 1977) have not yet been ratified by as many States as had been expected. By 31 May 1986, only 59 States Parties had ratified Protocol I and only 52 Protocol II. That proportion of ratifications over nine years is not negligible considering the long and protracted ratification procedures of many countries. But it was thought that there was a good chance of achieving universality as the Protocols merely adapted the 1949 Conventions which have been ratified by 163 States covering nearly the whole world.

80. So far, the Protocols have been ratified essentially by the Third World countries and neutral European and Nordic States. The other Western States (except France which has just ratified Protocol II) and East European States (except Yugoslavia) have not. It is encouraging to note that a great majority of States Parties are from the Third World. The diplomatic Conference of 1974-1977 which drafted the Protocols was the first conference of its kind where ex-colonies were able to put forward their own views and feelings and express their concerns about humanitarian law. It should also be noted that of the five permanent Members of the United Nations Security Council (which are also nuclear powers) only China has ratified both Protocols (France having ratified only Protocol II).

81. The reluctance to ratify Protocol I stems from the assimilation of wars of national liberation to international conflicts and the nearly complete prohibition of reprisals against civilians and civilian objects. This reluctance is even stronger among certain Powers because of the nuclear issue. On the subject of reprisals, all Protocol I does is to draw the logical conclusion from the recognized principle of protection of civilian populations; it in no way reformulates the nuclear issue which was clearly raised by international customary law and the principles of the universally accepted Conventions of 1949. Finally the Protocol does not in fact give a practical scope to wars of national liberation since decolonization has practically been completed and the relevant articles only apply to the concerned States which have ratified Protocol I.

82. Reluctance to ratify Protocol II also stems from the fear that it might jeopardize the sovereignty of newly independent States. A number of Third World countries feel that they might be deprived of the right to choose the appropriate means to deal with potential internal threats. The fear of undermining their newly acquired sovereignty, concern for territorial integrity, and the threat of foreign interference, are among the difficulties often evoked. Yet, this rather short instrument—which only contains 18 articles—has a very limited scope which is further restricted by the exclusion at the upper end of the scale of wars of national liberation and at the lower end of situations of internal disturbance and tension. It is therefore quite clear that the fear of Third World States about internal difficulties is quite unfounded.

83. Moreover Article 3 of Protocol II concerning intervention clearly states that no provision in the Protocol 'shall be invoked as a justification for the purpose of affecting the sovereignty of a State or the responsibility of the government, by all legitimate means, to maintain or re-establish law and order . . . or to defend the national unity and territorial integrity of the State'. The Diplomatic Conference even went so far as to omit any reference in the final text to the term 'Parties to the conflict' so that no provision of the Protocol could have any effect on the legal status of those Parties. Finally the Protocol was careful to avoid granting any privileged status or treatment to captured combatants. It is difficult therefore to see why Third World States would not massively ratify Protocol II.

84. Finally, it should be noted that in the case of internal conflicts, the Government itself has everything to gain by applying Protocol II. Since the Protocol has in fact improved the protection of victims of internal conflicts (which had only been briefly mentioned in common Article 3 of the 1949 Conventions) and specifically restricted its scope to conflicts between the State and insurgent forces controlling part of its territory, it would seem in the interest of both Parties to observe the rules over and above purely humanitarian considerations.

85. In order to encourage ratification of Protocol II, it is desirable that ICRC efforts be supported by international organizations. Regional organizations can play an important part as they have done to promote human rights. In that context the Independent Commission for its part sent a detailed memorandum to states which have not yet acceded to the Protocols, urging them to do so. The members of the Commission, independently and collectively, are continuing their efforts in this direction.

Furthermore it would be useful to make known some kind of 'interpretation' showing that the Protocol in no way challenges State sovereignty. It only refers to conflicts of high intensity, excludes situations of internal disturbances and tensions, does not grant opponents any legal status or special combatant treatment and only aims to protect civilian populations and rescue the injured and the sick. With that kind of assurance concerning the status of insurgents, the meaning of civilian protection and the scope of the Protocol, Third World States ought to be able to ratify the instrument more easily.

3. The need for a simpler expression of humanitarian principles applicable in armed conflicts

86. One of the reasons why humanitarian norms are not always observed is the complex or even esoteric character of the rules. It may therefore be useful to emphasize the fundamental principles of humanitarian law so that they can at any time be quite clear to any recipient. Thus isolated from the mass of rules of procedure and implementation, these principles would become perfectly 'visible' and their non-observance would also be readily apparent. The aim therefore would be to highlight the fundamental principles and eventually to annex to them the operational provisions in which they are at present drowned.

87. It was with this in mind that the President of the ICRC, Mr Alexandre Hay, suggested in 1975 the elaboration of a declaration summarizing simply the fundamental principles underlying humanitarian law in order to render them more visible and more easily understandable. Following this initiative, a group of ICRC experts drew up the draft 'Fundamental rules of international humanitarian law applicable in armed conflicts' (1979). The ICRC was able to summarize in a one-page document and in seven very specific points that corpus of rules, stating that

> the document summarizes the essential parts of this law. Its authors have endeavoured, as far as possible, to use simple and concise terms. These rules are not vested with the authority of an international legal instrument and are not intended to take the place of the treaties in force. Their sole purpose is to facilitate the dissemination of knowledge of international humanitarian law.

Obviously, these principles restated in a 'declaration' or a reminder should neither stop short of nor go beyond the existing conventional provisions. They should exactly reflect the content of existing treaty provisions and help them to be understood and publicized. The adoption or rather the endorsement or confirmation of these principles by an organ like the General Assembly of the United Nations in a resolution or even by the next International Conference of the Red Cross would unquestionably help reinforce their value for the protection of victims of armed conflicts which has already been recognized by the international community as a whole.

According to the text entitled 'Fundamental rules of international humanitarian law applicable in armed conflicts':

1. Persons *hors de combat* and those who do not take a direct part in hostilities are entitled to respect for their lives and physical and moral integrity. They shall in all circumstances be protected and treated

humanely without any adverse distinction.

2. It is forbidden to kill or injure an enemy who surrenders or who is *hors de combat*.

3. The wounded and sick shall be collected and cared for by the party to the conflict which has them in its power. Protection also covers medical personnel, establishments, transports and *matériel*. The emblem of the red cross or the red crescent is the sign of such protection and must be respected.

4. Captured combatants and civilians under the authority of an adverse party are entitled to respect for their lives, dignity, personal rights and convictions. They shall be protected against all acts of violence and reprisals. They shall have the right to correspond with their families and to receive relief.

5. Everyone shall be entitled to benefit from fundamental judicial guarantees. No one shall be held responsible for an act he has not committed. No one shall be subjected to physical or mental torture, corporal punishment or cruel or degrading treatment.

6. Parties to a conflict and members of their armed forces do not have an unlimited choice of methods and means of warfare. It is prohibited to employ weapons or methods of warfare of a nature to cause unnecessary losses or excessive suffering.

7. Parties to a conflict shall at all times distinguish between the civilian population and combatants in order to spare civilian population and property. Neither the civilian population as such nor civilian persons shall be the object of attack. Attacks shall be directed solely against military objectives.

4. The need for 'Principles applicable in any circumstances'

88. Beyond re-statement of the basic principles applicable to 'armed conflicts', the ICRC contemplated as early as 1971 another attempt to spell out the basic principles applicable not only to armed conflicts but in any circumstances (i.e. including situations of internal disturbances and tensions). Such a document would include a simplified formulation of the peremptory and intransgressible principles of humanitarian law already universally recognized as well as other rules still to be elaborated dealing with situations of internal disturbances and tensions. The document would therefore include rules governing the normal conduct of the State and the fundamental and intransgressible provisions of humanitarian law and human rights. The text would not, however, replace existing law. Its advantage would be to make the law more visible for those who are expected to carry it out in the field and to contribute to the universal recognition of fundamental humanitarian principles applicable in situations of internal disturbances and tensions which still remain outside the scope of humanitarian law.

5. Towards the elaboration of norms applicable to internal disturbances and tensions

89. There is undoubtedly a need for a special effort to bring within the context of humanitarian law situations of internal disturbances and tensions. Indeed, the gap must be filled urgently because of the importance of the matter but great caution must be exercised in view of its sensitive nature. Situations which are not covered by humanitarian law *stricto sensu* are however implicitly governed by declarations, international covenants and other human rights instruments as a whole. What has to be done in this case is to link human rights with humanitarian law which would represent a major step forward as regards the enquiry and control mechanisms. One should not of course be unduly optimistic in a field where States are particularly concerned about their sovereignty.

90. It would surely not be realistic to expect States to accept at the present time any binding instrument such as a convention dealing with the subject. They would regard this as a limitation of their domestic authority to maintain or re-establish law and order in their own territory. Perhaps it would be more realistic to elaborate within the United Nations a draft declaration on those situations along the lines of the United Nations Declaration on torture and to leave each State free to endorse through a 'unilateral declaration' the whole or part of this United Nations Declaration. Were the declaration to be violated by the endorsing State, the publicity given to the United Nations debate would constitute the kind of penalty a State would not willingly be subjected to. This is why it would be better to be even more modest in this regard.

The document to be elaborated could aim at ensuring the widest possible circulation of these rules of conduct, which is a particularly flexible way to make States and their officials observe minimum standards in situations of internal disturbances and tensions. The publicity given to such a text, especially if endorsed by an international forum, would give it a better chance of asserting itself in the conscience of mankind.

91. In any case, whatever the form and the legal status of the text, it is important to outline its possible content which should reflect the minimum requirements concerning the protection of the human person. Even if that content does not take the form of a diplomatic instrument, it would have the merit of representing a minimum standard and would serve as a yardstick for State behaviour. By its very existence, it would constitute a reference point, a sort of code of conduct for States.

92. Such a document would draw both on human rights and humanitarian law. It would reassert the need to observe at all times certain fundamental rules in the following fields:

- the right to life;
- dignity of the human person;
- no unlimited choice of the means used to maintain law and order;
- prohibition of acts of terrorism and of indiscriminate violence;
- prohibition of torture and degrading treatment;
- respect for the injured and protection of medical action;
- prohibition of forced or involuntary disappearances;
- fundamental judicial guarantees;
- special protection of children;
- dissemination and teaching of these fundamental rules.

93. It could be said that the adoption of this kind of text containing these points would be stimulated by concrete progress that could be achieved in the near future regarding the effective protection of the victims concerned. It might also appear that the adoption of the document would in itself represent the qualitative improvement sought to extend the legal coverage of situations of internal disturbances and tensions. The two objectives—effective protection and legal coverage—are, in fact, complementary.

Conclusion: Towards a realistic humanitarian strategy

94. While it may seem generally unrealistic to change, in the short and medium term, the most significant parameters of the international environment, it does not mean that the present situation, in particular the violations of humanitarian law, must simply be accepted. If humanitarian law is violated, it is not because it is useless: indeed, in the domestic context, no one can think that criminal law is useless just because it is violated by criminals. Non-observance does not amount to non-existence of law. Rather it highlights the need to reinforce it. In order to be really useful, a 'humanitarian strategy' must take the political environment into account. It would be useless to propose rules reflecting high humanitarian ideals which would be too far removed from reality to exert any real influence.

95. One of the elements in this context is that humanitarian law, which in the past was meant to apply to conventional warfare, has now to be applied to a great variety of sensitive and constantly changing internal and international situations. The recent development of the content of humanitarian norms is a reflection of the dramatic evolution of combat methods and their effects on civilian populations. The humanitarian strategy must take this into account.

96. Humanitarian law, updated in 1977 by the Additional Protocols, is particularly detailed, if not complete, and now rests on a few fundamental principles and rules of procedure and implementation. The updating process which essentially covered the protection of civilian populations showed the limits of what can be achieved in the present international context. It would therefore be in vain to build a humanitarian strategy based on the development of rules which have little chance of being universally accepted. Leaving aside the so-called technical gaps (war on land, neutrality, marking and identifying medical transport especially for war on the sea) which can be filled without fundamental changes or insurmountable political difficulties, there are two main gaps remaining: the prohibition of nuclear weapons and individual protection in situations of internal disturbances and tensions. At the present time, neither can be filled within the framework of the humanitarian strategy because multilateral diplomatic negotiations are apparently ruled out in the present state of international environment.

97. The prohibition of nuclear weapons, which is the absolute imperative of humanitarian law and a condition for its very existence, cannot be achieved in the framework of negotiation of humanitarian law, but rather in the context of disarmament. Whether one likes it or not, it is an inescapable fact that only negotiations between the nuclear powers can achieve any results following a process of disarmament discussions which have been going on for quite some time now and will probably have to continue for a considerable period. The reinforcement and even the credibility of humanitarian law depend on a number of factors and variables which it can hardly control. Conversely, however, if humanitarian law is able to devise an appropriate formulation of its concerns regarding the nuclear issue, it cannot fail in the long run to have a considerable impact on disarmament negotiations.

98. As for the application of humanitarian law to less intense internal conflicts in the form of situations of internal disturbances and tensions, it cannot be achieved by a treaty-based limitation of State sovereignty: no State would ever be prepared to accept this and no humanitarian organization would or should ever call for such a solution. A better humanitarian control of this type of situation can only be ensured in the present context by a flexible reminder of a series of minimum rules combining both human rights and humanitarian law. One of the components of the humanitarian strategy is therefore to encourage States to ratify the International Covenants on Human Rights. The drafting of a 'code of conduct' listing minimum norms to be observed could lead, in the more or less distant future in a favourable international climate, to some kind of a standard declaration. This would be subject to a certain form of approval which it would be unwise to try to specify or outline at this stage.

99. The question of the methods and means of controlling the implementation of humanitarian law is both difficult and alarming. Strategy cannot lose sight of reality, i.e. of the fact that any form of control is too closely dependent on State consent. One of the means of action of the strategy is to call on States to sign the declaration under Article 90 of Protocol I, by which they would recognize the powers of the International Fact Finding Commission. This Commission will only come into effect when 20 States Parties to the Protocols have made that declaration. So far only seven States have done so, the four neutral European States (Austria, Finland, Sweden, Switzerland), as well as Denmark, Norway and Italy.

100. Equally important as a means of control is the role played by publicity. The ICRC has the possibility of public appeals in cases of serious and repeated violations which have not ceased after its intervention, if it appears that ICRC delegates have witnessed such violations or that they are well known and if the ICRC is satisfied that publicity may benefit the victims.

101. Public opinion has proved an efficient instrument in the field of human rights. At a time when man's link to the world is dependent on the media, the media have a vital role to play in public information and awareness.

102. It is regrettable that violations of humanitarian law do not arouse as much public interest as violations of human rights, since human dignity is at stake in both cases. In humanitarian law, there is no equivalent to the kind of annual report by Amnesty International. There are far fewer bodies concerned with denouncing breaches of humanitarian norms.

103. Likewise, it is important to highlight the position of journalists on dangerous professional missions. At present, they do not enjoy sufficient safeguards to protect and facilitate the exercise of their missions. They are referred to in Protocol I but not in Protocol II. Mistrusted by States and poorly protected by law, journalists often have to take considerable risks and pay a high price to do their work. This has been illustrated recently by a number of tragic cases. There is room for improvement in this field and greater efforts are undoubtedly called for.

104. Publicity may be one of the constitutive elements of control conferred on the United Nations under Article 89 of the Protocol I which provides for an actual *actio popularis*. There is therefore yet another reason to encourage States to ratify that Protocol.

105. Interestingly enough, in the field of control, despite great expressions of shyness in these times of expanding State sovereignty, humanitarian law does sometimes include a few rather bold provisions. Apart from the sort of *actio popularis* provided by common Article 1 of the 1949 Geneva Conventions under which States are not only bound to respect but to ensure respect for the Conventions, there is also Article 89 of Protocol I which calls on States to act, jointly or individually, in co-operation with the United Nations to ensure respect for humanitarian law. In the same spirit, in one of its appeals the ICRC stated that:

> Any government which, while not itself involved in a conflict, is in a position to exert a deterrent influence on a government violating the laws of war, but refrains from doing so, shares the responsibility for the breaches. By failing to react while able to do so, it fosters the process which could lead to its becoming the victim of similar breaches and no longer an accessory by omission.[15]

This is in fact a very strongly worded statement particularly in view of the use of the notion of shared responsibility. As far as we know, this is the first time State responsibility is formally mentioned for an act committed by another State. It is also the first time that the obligation to come to the rescue of persons in peril which exists in municipal law has been mentioned in international law.

106. The control of respect for humanitarian norms is still too dependent on consensus and therefore on the political will of States. It was thought that a mission of jurisdictional control could be entrusted to the International Court of Justice. But neither the 1949 Geneva Conventions nor Protocol I relating to international conflicts explicitly gave the Court this power. To bring a case before the Court a special jurisdictional link based on Article 36 of the International Court's Statute would be required which takes us back to square one, i.e. State consent. The resolution of the 1949 Diplomatic Conference calling upon States to submit to the Court their disputes on the interpretation or application of the 1949 Geneva Conventions is not enough to establish the Court's jurisdiction under Article 36 of its Statute.

107. So we are left with a humanitarian law intended for man but dependent on the State: such is the inescapable paradox. We should not regard the excessive dependence on State consent as a major obstacle, for the State itself has evolved. In particular its pivotal role in international relations has undergone a considerable change. The State used to be the sole actor in the international order. Institutional and normative mechanisms made it the sole responsible entity in internal matters, allowing no external interference.

The double role of the State, as the only subject of international law and as the unique actor for internal matters, is now contested. The final recipient of the norms of humanitarian law is not the State but the individual. The 'Prince' of yore with his supreme *auctoritas* and *potestas* is increasingly becoming a mere link transmitting rules elaborated above him to individuals below him. This process gives international law in general and humanitarian law in particular its essential finality, i.e. the service of mankind. The State is not alone in contributing to this end. The international community also does so because man ultimately represents the common heritage of humanity. The State is only justified by the justice it guarantees mankind. Justice reinforces the State, and without justice the State destroys itself. Saint Augustin noted that a bunch of criminals, like the State, is a group of men led by a chief held together by mutual consent and the observance of certain rules in the sharing of the loot. And Saint Augustin recalled the answer given by the pirate to Alexander the Great who had asked him what right he had to roam the seas: 'The same right you have to roam the world. Because I use a small vessel I am called a pirate, and because you use a fleet you are called an emperor.' It is only by respecting justice and the human person that the State can and must find its justification. If not, the State as a political association is nothing better than a bunch of criminals. The best way therefore for the State to succeed is for humanitarianism to succeed. Political and humanitarian considerations are not irreconcilable; far from it. In fact, they reinforce one another. As Sophocles put it in Antigone: 'There are many wonders in the world but none is more wonderful than man.'

Notes

1. Gaston Bouthoul, 'La Guerre', Paris, PUF, coll. Que sais-je?, 1953, p.8.
2. Gaston Bouthoul, ibid, p.109-110.
3. Charles de Gaulle, 'Du prestige', Revue militaire francaise, juin 1931.
4. Albert Einstein and Sigmund Freud, 'Why War?', International Institute of Intellectual Co-operation, League of Nations, Geneva, 1933, p.8.
5. Albert Camus, 'Actuelles I', Chroniques algaceriennes, Paris, éd. Gallimard, 1958, p.24.
6. 'International dimensions of humanitarian law', Institut Henry Dunant, Geneve, UNESCO and Pèdone, 1986, in particular the first part relating to the contribution of different cultures and traditions and the different trends of African, Asian, Socialist, Islamic, Latin-American and Western thought. More than 3,200 years ago, the Egypto-Hittite peace treaty of 1,278 B.C. provided a blueprint for the humanization of relations in times of war (see text in the 'Revue générale de droit international public', Paris, 1941-1945, p.35). Also Henri Pirenne, the Belgian historian, who wrote: 'Towns which were captured were no longer destroyed, populations which had been defeated were no longer massacred, pillage had given way to a war levy.' (H Pirenne, 'Les grands courants de l'histoire universelle', I, Neuchâtel, 1959, p.91).
7. 'The efforts of ICRC in the case of violations of international

humanitarian law', The International Review of the Red Cross, March–April 1981.

8. Maurice Torrelli, 'Le droit international humanitaire', Paris, PUF, Coll. 'Que sais-je?', 1985, p.7-14.

9. Jean Pictet, 'Développement et principes du droit international humanitaire' Geneve, Institut Henry Dunant and Paris, Pèdone, 1983, p.107.

10. International Military Tribunal, Trial of the Major Criminals, Nuremberg, 14 November/1 October 1946, Nuremberg, 1947, vol. 1, p.253-254.

11. ICRC, Report to the XXI International Conference of the Red Cross, 'Reaffirmation and development of the laws and customs in armed conflicts', Geneva, May 1969, p.64.

12. Roger Pinto, 'Le droit des relations internationales', Paris, Payot, 1972, p.313-315.

13. See J. P. Charnay, 'De la dégradation du droit des gens', Paris.

14. ICRC, 'Respect for and development of international humanitarian law. From Manila (1981) to Geneva (1986): interim assessment and future prospects', Geneva, January 1985, p.18.

15. Published in the International Review of the Red Cross, January–February 1985 and September-October 1985.

Statement made at the Plenary Meeting of the Independent Commission, New York, November 1983.

Alexandre Hay*

Mr. Chairman, Excellencies,

I am glad to be able to address such a gathering of eminent individuals concerned with the increasingly grave humanitarian problems of our time.

The International Committee of the Red Cross (ICRC) has, for the last 120 years, served the cause of humanity in a world torn by conflicts.

In 1864, a year after the ICRC was founded, the Geneva Convention for the Amelioration of the Condition of the Wounded in Armies in the Field, the first multilateral humanitarian law treaty, established a legal basis for ICRC activities and brought about the recognition of the Red Cross movement by the States.

Growing from ten articles in 1864 to some six hundred today, humanitarian law has made progress and ICRC activities have developed along with it, the one promoting the other.

The 1864 Convention afforded protection only to the wounded and sick soldiers of armies in the field; after the naval battle of Tsoushima, it was adapted in 1907 to sea warfare.

After the First World War, in the course of which the ICRC assisted and protected hundreds of thousands of prisoners of war, a new convention formally extended ICRC protection to prisoners of war.

---

* Alexandre Hay is President of the International Committee of the Red Cross

The tragic experiences of the Spanish Civil War and of the Second World War led to a recasting of the Geneva Conventions in 1949 and widened their scope in two ways:

1. Four Conventions, which still constitute the basis of current humanitarian law:
   i) the First, affording protection to wounded and sick soldiers;
   ii) the Second, affording protection to shipwrecked members of armed forces;
   iii) the Third, dealing with prisoners of war;
   iv) the Fourth, a new one, dealing with civilians.

2. Article 3 common to the four Conventions, a kind of mini-Convention affording protection to victims of non-international armed conflicts.

The war in Algeria, the war in Vietnam, and all the armed struggles for independence showed both the practical value and also the limits of the four 1949 Conventions. Its achievements, and also the obstacles it encountered in helping the victims of these conflicts, led the ICRC to convene, in 1971 and 1972, two conferences of government experts to examine proposals for up-dating humanitarian law.

In 1977, a Diplomatic Conference, presided over by Federal Councillor Graber who is also a member of this Commission, adopted two Protocols additional to the 1949 Conventions: Protocol I affording protection to the victims of international armed conflicts and Protocol II protecting the victims of non-international armed conflicts. These two Protocols broke new ground in the field of contemporary humanitarian law: protection of civilians against the effects of hostilities, classification of wars of national liberation as international armed conflicts, extension of protection to combatants in guerrilla warfare.

Emmanuel Mounier said that 'Law is always a precarious attempt to subjugate force to reason and to turn it towards love'. He added: 'But it is also a struggle!'

This struggle is fought by the ICRC mainly in the field, in the heart of conflicts, alongside the victims of such conflict. Today, the ICRC maintains about thirty delegations with 400 delegates, who are active in some 70 countries, with regular and special annual budgets of the order of a hundred million dollars (one-third for the regular budget and two-thirds for specially financed activities), serving primarily for the protection of, but also for assistance to, a growing number of victims of armed conflicts and internal troubles and tensions.

The Geneva Conventions of 1949 and the Protocol I of 1977, provide for the following safeguards to ensure the rights of the victims of armed conflicts:

* the primary responsibility of the Party States;
* the institution of the Protecting Power;
* the role of the ICRC in assistance and protection and, in the field of assistance, that of the Red Cross and Red Crescent movement;
* the role of the United Nations;
* the establishment of an International Fact-Finding Commission;
* the procedures of enquiry, (Article. 52 of Convention I, 53 of Convention II, 132 of Convention I and 149 of Convention IV).

According to Article 1 common to the 1949 Conventions and Protocol I 'The High Contracting Parties undertake to respect and to ensure respect for the Conventions and Protocols in all circumstances.' The Party States therefore have a dual responsibility, that of applying the stipulated provisions themselves, as well as a collective responsibility for ensuring their respect by other States even though no formal procedure for doing so has been stipulated.

The Protecting Power is a state, neutral or non-party to the conflict, which, nominated by one party to the conflict and accepted by the opposing party, is prepared to undertake the task of safeguarding the interests of the party to the conflict which nominated it. Its role basically is to supervise the condition of prisoners of war and interned civilians, parallel to ICRC's activities in this domain.

Since 1949, the only cases when a Protecting Power was nominated concerned Switzerland in the Suez conflict in 1956, the Goa conflict in 1961 and the war between India and Pakistan in 1971-1972, although in the last case the mandate Switzerland received was not interpreted in the same way by both parties.

The role of the International Committee of the Red Cross, in accordance with the 1949 Geneva Conventions and the 1977 Protocols is, generally speaking, to serve as a neutral intermediary between parties to conflicts in order to bring protection and assistance to the victims.

More specifically, this entails the following activities:

* to visit and interview without witness prisoners of war (Article 126 of the Third Convention) and detained or interned civilians (Articles 76 and 143 of the Fourth Convention);
* to provide aid to the populations of occupied territories (Articles 59 and 61 of the Fourth Convention);
* to look for missing persons and transmit family messages to prisoners of war (Article 123 of the Third Convention) and to civilians (Article 140 of the Fourth Convention);
* to offer its services in the establishment of hospital zones and localities (Article 123 of the Third Convention) and security zones and localities (Article 14 of the Fourth Convention);
* to receive requests for aid from protected persons (Article 30 of the Fourth Convention);
* to exercise its right of initiative; this means that it may ask the parties to a conflict to agree to its discharging other humanitarian functions in the event of non-international armed conflicts (Article 3 common to the four Geneva Conventions of 1949) and international armed conflicts (Article 9 of the First, Second and Third Conventions, and Article 10 of the Fourth Convention);
* to act, wherever necessary, as a substitute for the Protecting Power.

The assistance of the Red Cross in general, and, in particular, of the National Societies and their federation, the League, is defined by a general clause in Protocol I, Article 81.

The role of the United Nations is mentioned in Article 89 of Protocol I: 'In situations of serious violations of the Conventions or of this Protocol, the High Contracting Parties undertake to act, jointly or individually, in co-operation with the United Nations and in conformity with the United Nations Charter.'

The facultative formation of an International Fact-Finding Commission was introduced, on a proposal by Sweden, in Article 90 of Protocol I. This Commission shall be convened when twenty High Contracting Parties have agreed to accept its competence.

All in all, it can be said that the international community today has an updated body of international law applicable in case of armed conflict, together with the procedures for its implementation.

It should be pointed out, however, that as this law has been developed, and the number of its implementation procedures increased, the number of obstacles to its implementation has also increased.

In the worsening international climate there is a growing tendency to resort to force, both between and within States, increasing the number of conflicts as well as the number of victims.

Confronted with the present crises, governments are tempted to think only in the short term, to reject everything that does not fit in with immediate interests, and to relegate humanitarian considerations to second place behind what they consider to be the imperatives of politics and security.

This refusal to implement humanitarian law defies the whole international community (the States, the legal system, the organizations) and inflicts intolerable suffering on the victims of conflicts.

In 1981, at the 24th International Red Cross Conference in Manila, I said how concerned the ICRC was at the escalation of indiscriminate violence, the repeated violation of basic humanitarian principles, the politicization of humanitarian law and the arms race in a starving world.

The International Red Cross Conference adopted two resolutions (Resolutions IV and VI) reminding all parties to conflicts of their humanitarian obligations. The first of these two resolutions deplored the fact that the ICRC had been refused access to captured combatants and civilian detainees in the armed conflicts of Western Sahara, Ogaden and Afghanistan. It was no coincidence that these three situations were mixed conflicts, being both internal and international, whose legal status had political implications liable to jeopardize humanitarian action for the benefit of the victims of the conflicts.

Two years after Manila, these refusals still stand, except in the case of Ogaden, and the list, regrettably, is not complete. It would be remiss of me not to remind you of the ICRC appeal last May to the whole international community as well as to Iraq and Iran concerning our activities in those two warring countries. Nor should I omit our repeated approaches to Israel to secure its recognition of the applicability of the Fourth Convention to the occupied territories and to ensure respect of the Convention in all areas.

Besides operating in situations of armed conflict, the ICRC, with the consent of the governments concerned, visits persons detained as a result of internal troubles and tensions. Since the end of the Second World War, the ICRC has visited more than 300,000 detainees in eighty countries.

But in numerous situations which are not covered by the 1949 Geneva Conventions and their 1977 Protocols, the ICRC was not allowed access to persons detained as a result of serious troubles.

As the initiator of the Red Cross movement and of humanitarian law, the ICRC works unceasingly to help innocent victims of conflicts and to foster the humanitarian spirit in action and in law.

Over the last few years, the ICRC has seen its activities expand despite certain setbacks, and has also witnessed an increased need for all kinds of support to undertake operations wherever possible and to overcome obstacles.

On the outbreak of the armed conflict between Iraq and Iran, the ICRC reminded both parties of the applicability of the Geneva Conventions. It set up or strengthened its delegations in Baghdad and Teheran and maintained a constant dialogue with the authorities. Prompted by the numerous difficulties we came up against, I myself carried out several missions to both Baghdad and Teheran in order to meet the leaders of both countries. Since these discreet steps proved insufficient, the ICRC launched a public appeal to the two parties and to all the States bound by the Geneva Conventions.

On a general level, the ICRC has for several months been in touch with several governments and independent specialists on the matter of how to enforce humanitarian law and its underlying principles.

In 1984, the ICRC will step up these experts' consultations and will pursue them further in 1985 and 1986. The aim should be to foster awareness of this problem, having in mind the 25th International Red Cross Conference in Geneva in 1986.

To this end, the ICRC would gladly continue its discussions with the Commission or those of its members who are best informed on this subject.

The purpose of these discussions should be to agree with these specialists on ways of:

a) improving knowledge of and respect for humanitarian law, not only in military circles, but also and above all among politicians in positions of authority;

b) drawing the attention of parties to conflicts, and all the States bound by the Geneva Conventions to the existence in the Conventions and Protocols of procedures for their application (including the institution of Protecting Powers) and encouraging them to make use of such procedures to implement humanitarian law.

Even though this renewed affirmation of existing law and the procedures for its application is a matter of urgent concern and high priority, it should not exclude new developments.

As a matter of fact, several areas were left untouched when humanitarian law was recently supplemented. The ICRC has begun to consider improving the humanitarian rules governing, among other things, the following problems: sea warfare, neutrality, lawful methods and means of combat, medical transport, etc., to mention only a few areas where better protection of human beings in times of conflict seems to us to be necessary. In the near future, the ICRC will approach experts and States for consultations on these various topics.

The situation of the individual caught up in violence in a State, violence that ranges from simple internal tensions to more serious internal disturbances, is a cause of deep concern to the ICRC. A suggestion was made recently to draft a declaration of basic and inalienable rights applicable to cases of collective violence within States, in situations that would not already be covered by humanitarian law. The ICRC considers this idea worth pursuing and intends to examine it during its consultations with experts.

Mr. Chairman, Excellencies, the main questions I would like to put to you today are these: how should one go about stimulating this awareness of humanitarian values among political leaders? How should one foster the humanitarian spirit in politics? How can one demonstrate that in every political situation there are humanitarian aspects which one ignores at one's peril?

We, who are every day confronted with the victims' plight, would be grateful should you be able, with your command of political affairs, to conceive of ways and means to promote the acceptance and application of humanitarian law and its principles among political leaders and to bring awareness to public opinion.

With your experience and standing, you have access to most political leaders and you can urge:

a) the speedy ratification of the Additional Protocols, which are a basic supplement to humanitarian law in its main areas such as the protection of civilians against hostilities;

b) a better knowledge of the existing instruments of humanitarian law;

c) the faithful application of these instruments in all circumstances, and full cooperation with existing humanitarian organizations;

d) a better use of the institutions and procedures provided for in existing statutory law: collective responsibility of the States party to the Conventions, Protecting Power, Fact-Finding Commission.

We should not forget that there are also questions of mediation between parties to conflicts, between States or within States, nor should we forget limited but especially acute problems, such as that of missing or stateless persons.

The ideal would evidently be to reach the stage where humanitarian principles would be so much a matter of course that there would be no need for humanitarian institutions or law. But we are still a long way from achieving this.

Mr. Chairman, Excellencies, there are many other problems that ought to be mentioned, so many tragic and admirable cases on which to report. We could speak of them far longer.

For the moment, I would like to conclude with the wish that we may all continue to do our share for humanity wherever we may be of most service, supporting each other and restoring a little peace and solidarity to a world that so sorely needs it.

Statement* made at the Plenary Meeting of the Independent Commission, Stockholm, May 1986.

Jacques Moreillon**

It's indeed a pleasure and an honour for me to be here today with you and share with you some of the concerns of the International Committee of the Red Cross about the forthcoming International Red Cross Conference which is going to take place in October in Geneva this year. As you are aware, the International Conference of the Red Cross takes place, in principle, every four years. The last one was in Manila, in 1981. Actually, it's five years ago. This time is the first time since 1925 that it is taking place in Geneva. In the past it has taken place in all parts of the world in order to show the universality of the Red Cross and Red Crescent movement.

The Conference is the great humanitarian meeting of the world community. It gets together the representatives of over 150 States Parties to the Geneva Conventions of 1949. It also gets together over 135 national Red Cross or Red Crescent societies recognized by the ICRC, plus, of course, their federation, the League of Red Cross and Red Crescent Societies and the ICRC.

I think, if we want to go to the essentials, we may consider that there will be three major themes at that Conference which are likely to interest your Commission and I would say also the countries to which each of you belong.

One theme will be the revision of the statutes of the International Red Cross, including the change of the name, which would become

---

* Based on the verbatim record of the plenary meeting, Stockholm—May 1986.
** Jacques Moreillon is Director General of the International Committee of the Red Cross.

51

the International Red Cross and Red Crescent Movement. The second theme will be the ratification of the Additional Protocols to the Geneva Conventions, and the third, the activities of ICRC and the problems relating to the respect of humanitarian law. More specifically, we will try to strike a balance between the various results we have been able to achieve and the difficulties we have known in the conflict areas of the world.

What the ICRC plans to do, in the speech which President Hay will make in Commission I, under point 2.1 of the agenda, is to try and share with the world community, what I would call the positive and negative elements of these respective situations, because there is not a general image which comes from them. Some are relatively positive in humanitarian terms. Some are blocked today but may be loosened or improved between now and the Conference. Some are totally blocked and we see no light of hope for the time being. But all of this can evolve between now and that date and we hope will evolve positively, particularly in view of the upcoming Conference.

We consider that this will be a unique occasion for what we call a humanitarian mobilization through which we hope to get governments and also public opinion to understand (I would say) the political importance of solving humanitarian problems, in the sense that it is our conviction that humanitarian problems are not only humanitarian, and that an unsolved humanitarian problem indeed becomes a political one. One might use the formula that unsolved humanitarian problems are without pity for those who do not solve them. They tend, in fact, to deteriorate and take on a political dimension which makes them much harder to solve.

Sometimes the fact that humanitarian organizations are present is used by governments as an excuse not to seek the necessary solutions. As President Hay indicated to your Commission already in New York, when he first spoke to you, we have the feeling that humanitarian organizations tend to become a bit too much the 'pretext' of governments for not solving political problems.

We cannot claim, as humanitarian organizations, to modify the cause of problems. Perhaps to a certain extent by a humanitarian attitude we can bring a certain détente to a situation which induces not peace but a spirit of peace that might facilitate political solutions. That said, the Red Cross cannot, and should not itself propose political solutions.

The Red Cross is a rather special movement in the sense that it finds its strength within its limits. It is because we do not condemn aggression that we can visit the prisoners in the hands of the aggressor. It is because we do not ask for the liberation of political detainees that we can visit the political detainee and improve his lot. It is because we don't tell a government you should liberate Mr So and So that we can tell the government: you should treat Mr So and So better.

There is a very fundamental notion of finding strength within the knowledge of one's own limitations. The Red Cross is neither a judge nor the conscience of the world and humanity. It exists in order to assist and protect whenever given the possibility to do so. But, at the same time, if it is not given that possibility, then, indeed, matters escape the hands of government and by growing worse and worse become political problems.

If you reflect upon the essential nature of the law of war, for instance, of the law of armed conflicts, what is the first law of war, if not the right to kill? In a conflict between States, killing a military man belonging to the army of the enemy is not a crime, as long as this person is in uniform and fighting. From that point of view, at the heart of humanitarian law or the law of war, there is this fundamental notion that one must distinguish between the combatant and the non-combatant which implies in itself the acceptance not of war as a phenomenon, but of war as something which the international community has not been able to suppress until now. After all, the Geneva Conventions become 'alive', so to speak, when a conflict starts. It is not up to humanitarian law to determine whether a conflict is just or unjust. But once the conflict has started, the law sets a limit to this licence to kill.

What is this limit? It is, fundamentally, the distinction between combatant and non-combatant. In wartime, attacking a military objective, whether a building or a person, is legal. It's not our heart's desire, it's a fact of international law. But attacking civilians, the wounded, the sick, the Red Cross, the priests, the doctors, the shipwrecked—this is illegal. What is the common denominator between these various factors if not the fact that they are all non-combatants? Humanitarian law needs 600 articles to explain it, but basically it's not such a complicated affair. It is essentially the notion that one must spare those who cannot or can no longer fight. That is either the civilians or the wounded military men; the sick, the prisoners who are hors de combat, no longer able to fight. We consider that if we could get both governments and public opinion to respect that concept, it would indeed be a major step forward in the sensitization of public consciousness that not everything is allowed in terms of conflict.

From that point of view, the question of the ratification of the Additional Protocols to the Geneva Conventions is very important. What is the essence of the Protocols? Here again, there are about 120 articles, but the essence of the Protocols is simply that they prohibit attacks on civilians as such during the fighting. Basically, humanitarian law or the law of war is divided into two branches: the so-called law of Geneva and the so-called law of The Hague.

The Geneva law deals with what happens after the conflict: for example, to civilians who are interned or protected in occupied territories—on the basis of the IV Geneva Convention—the great missing convention in the Second World War. It's a tragedy of history that the ICRC proposed in 1935 to have a convention protecting civilians, whether interned or in occupied territories. The date fixed for that Convention was 1940. Of course, history caught up with that. What happens after the conflict to the military? The III Geneva Convention of 1929—of 1949 also, but it was born in 1929—protects the military, the prisoner of war who is hors de combat. It's after the conflict.

The law of The Hague regulates the conduct of hostilities. After the Second World War, the ICRC tried to introduce in the Geneva Conventions certain elements of the law of The Hague, such as, for instance, the prohibition from attacking civilians as such. But we were too early. After the Second World War everyone remember not only Hiroshima but Dresden and the V-2s over London and the mass bombing of civilian populations. It was inopportune, both for the victors and the vanquished, to prohibit practices which had been followed so much during the war. It took the world community twenty years, and to a certain extent the Vietnam war, to be able to raise the level of consciousness of public opinion and governmental opinion to obtain, in the Additional Protocols of 1974-77, the total prohibition of attacking civilians as such. Under the Chairmanship of President Graber, I think we achieved a major gain by obtaining such a prohibition.

Look at the conflict between Iraq and Iran today, at the question of the bombing of civilian populations which appeared some time ago. Look also at much of the conflict in Lebanon. In a way, what is terrorism but indiscriminate violence against non-guilty or against innocent victims? Indiscriminate violence against innocent victims is exactly what the Protocols prohibit, by saying: should you launch an attack, aim at the military. We feel that it is essential that these Protocols achieve as wide a ratification as possible.

We do not intend to use the October Conference to debate the merits of the Protocols. But we do intend to use it as a general encouragement to obtain universal ratification. 58 countries is a nice number but, still, it's a small number compared to the 155 which we have for the Geneva Conventions. We consider that universality of the Protocols should be as general as that of the Conventions.

Lastly, Mr Chairman, a word about the revision of the Statutes of the International Red Cross. The International Red Cross is a rather special body because it existed over fifty years of its life without statutes. This is due to historical circumstances. What happened on the battlefield of Solferino, when Henry Dunant started to tend the wounded there, was really the simultaneous invention of two ideas that are a tremendous success story. The basic idea of Henry Dunant was: a) the wounded must be respected and treated; and b) one should organize oneself already in time of peace to treat them when war comes. Out of a) the Geneva Conventions were born; out of b) the Red Cross and Red Crescent movement was born. Why? Because you need, if you want to go on a battlefield to treat the wounded, a treaty whereby you are protected while treating the wounded, and you need a distinctive sign to distinguish you from those who are there for fighting. The treaty was the Geneva Conventions, the distinctive sign was the Red Cross.

At that time, the International Committee of the Red Cross which, as you all know, is international in its activity but mononational in its structure, was the only co-ordinating organ of the movement. It was at the same time, I would say, the father and mother of those national societies which it recognized, in giving them legal birth. After the First World War, with Wilson's ideals and the concept that that was 'the war to end all wars', the notion came that with the League of Nations one had found a way to talk oneself out of war. Therefore, it was no longer necessary to have these national societies prepare themselves for conflict. And one had to create the equivalent, in Red Cross terms, of the League of Nations, namely the League of Red Cross Societies.

It was absolutely normal to consider that there should be a federation of these national societies for acting in time of peace. But in order to regulate the relationship between that new body, the League, the old co-ordinating body, the International Committee of the Red Cross, and the national societies, one needed statutes. And these were the statutes, the first statutes of the International Red Cross as adopted in 1928. As a result of the birth of the League, it had become necessary to create such statutes.

These statutes basically said: the ICRC will deal with warlike situations, armed conflicts, and the League will deal with peacetime situations. The ICRC will be the neutral intermediary, which is required in any conflict; the League will be the co-ordinator, which is required for the development of national societies and assistance in natural disasters. These statutes were slightly updated in 1952 and are being updated at the next International Conference of the Red Cross, basically without much difference in terms of substance. The name is going to be changed. Also, *one is giving* more weight to national societies. There is no article on the national societies in the present statute of the International Red Cross. *One is* foreseeing an article on the role of States which indicates more clearly, I would say, the positive relationship of mutual respect between States and the International Red Cross and Red Crescent movement: respect on the part of States for the fundamental principles of the Red Cross Movement and respect on the part of the Movement for the sovereignty of States. From that point of view, we consider that these statutes are an improvement upon, but not a fundamental step beyond, the present situation.

Of course, we will not change the reality that national societies are different from country to country. They are very much the expression of a certain situation in given countries. They tend to reflect the general social situation of respective countries. From that point of view, one must realize that the universality of the movement is bought to a certain extent at the cost of a considerable diversity, which we wish to maintain.

Coming back to the law of war, the main problem is to ensure compliance with, rather than development of, the existing law. If the States would only observe the rules which have already been laid down, 80% of our problems would be solved. Observance of the existing body of law is a more important issue than further development of it. Governments and peoples should not be led to believe that more law could be a remedy. What is needed is greater political will to comply with the existing norms.

The ultimate aim is to save the lives of men, women and children. The law is no more than a means to that end. It is certainly not an end in itself. At times it can even be an obstacle.

Strictly speaking, internal disturbances and tensions are not armed conflicts and therefore do not come within the purview of the Geneva Conventions. It is important to keep in mind that governments have no obligations with regard to the ICRC. As far as we are concerned, we do not wish to jeopardize the effective possibility we have enjoyed since World War II to visit political detainees all over the world. Our delegates have been able to see over half a million prisoners in 90 countries from Chile to Poland, from Asia and Africa to Ireland, without any legal basis, without the States having the slightest obligation to let us into their prisons. This is indeed a small miracle! The reasons of States for accepting our offers of service were certainly not legal reasons. We go to them and say: 'You have no obligation to accept the offer we are going to make. Our aim is strictly humanitarian. Legally, you may accept or refuse, but we do believe that there is a convergence of interests between the humanitarian aim to ensure adequate treatment of political prisoners and the political concern of your government to present a positive image to the outside world.' We may not put things quite so bluntly, but that is indeed how the message is understood and perceived.

What must be encouraged, with regard to internal disturbances and tensions, is an overall assessment which is not limited to the ICRC alone. It could take place on a regional basis, within the Organization of American States, the Organization of African Unity, the League of Arab States, the Council of Europe, one day perhaps within the United Nations. The aim would be to establish not a body of legal rules but a code of conduct—a few fundamental norms to be observed in situations of internal disturbances and tensions.

But these basic norms should not be connected with the humanitarian action of the ICRC. We do not wish to establish a link which would enable States to reject humanitarian action on the basis of their refusal to be associated with the fundamental norms. That would threaten humanitarian action which must be preserved at all costs. It is essential to prevent the establishment of any new law which in effect would go against the victims' interests.

Finally, with regard to current developments, we must decide whether to take a pessimistic view of things or adopt a different attitude. The ICRC has wondered how far it should go in issuing its warning. What we have done in the end is to try and strike a balance. We cannot pretend that all is for the best in the best of all possible worlds. To follow Candide's example would be both naive and wrong. But at the same time we should not generate despair and be entirely negative. We must achieve what we have called 'humanitarian mobilization' and show that it is both humanly possible and politically wise to be humanitarian. This enables us to strike the deepest human chord—I mean, a common human denominator which binds humanity together. Ultimately our approach is that humanitarian ideals and political concerns are not incompatible.

We must realize that for a decade or so conflicts have intensified and become longer, reaching a kind of stalemate.

In the Western Saharan conflict, prisoners of war have been held for ten years, twice as long as in World War II. In the Ogaden, some prisoners have been held for nine years. For the refugees on the Thai-Kampuchean border, the situation has taken on a Palestinian flavour of permanence. Why? Because the political problem has not been tackled. The Iran-Iraq war has lasted longer than World War II. Situations are of course becoming more complex, but ideologies are also hardening.

In our view, there are two main challenges to be faced by the year 2000. The first is to find some form of common language with extremists on all sides, with people who have opted out of human universality because their own truth is too absolute to accommodate any other. While this is a feature of our time, it is not necessarily without precedent. We may recall the Wars of Religion or the Inquisition. Indeed we have no lessons to give, in the recent or the more distant past. One of the forms of radicalization is of course the emergence of terrorism and one of the major issues for the future is how to deal with the radicalization of ideologies.

The second challenge is to learn to live in a certain chaos. What

I mean is that, perhaps because of the proliferation of texts or because of the different perceptions of law in different parts of the world, legal norms are being increasingly flouted. This does not mean that we should not try to hold on to them. Indeed we are the first to welcome the existence of such instruments as the Geneva Conventions when they can be invoked. But we must face up to the fact that legal norms are no longer observed the way they used to be.

Power structures have changed. We no longer know who is in charge in a country, who to contact for a particular purpose. There are many complex reasons for this change, and we do not have the time to go into more detail. But the fact is that we are living in a form of permanent chaos and to survive we must above all hold on to certain fundamental principles and find the deepest and most common features of mankind. Not that the law should be rejected and replaced by mere principles, but we should embark on a synthesizing effort to find, circulate and publicize our common denominators. And the first common denominator is the fact that we all are human beings.

It is this deepest, perhaps even subliminal, chord that must be struck in our future programme.

Respect of Humanitarian Norms in International Conflicts

Interstate wars and wars of national liberation

Georges Abi-Saab

Contents

Georges Abi-Saab is Professor of International Law and Organization, Graduate Institute of International Studies, Geneva. He was a member of the Egyptian delegation to the Diplomatic Conference on the Reaffirmation and Development of International Humanitarian Law. He is the author of several books and studies in international law and in particular in the field of humanitarian law.

2. Fragmenting the function of the Protecting Power and multiplying the substitutes.
3. Activating the collective responsibility of the Parties in the observance of the Conventions and the Protocols.

V Wars of national liberation

Introduction

Lauterpacht once wrote: 'If international law is the vanishing point of law, the law of war is the vanishing point of international law'. Indeed, at first glance, the traditional denomination of this field of law, the law of war, seems a contradiction in terms; for how can 'law' which is an ordered pattern for social interaction, co-exist with or regulate 'war', which is a radical break-down of all social order between the belligerents? The new denomination is no less paradoxical. The terms 'humanitarian law' and 'armed conflict' evoke contradictory rather than complementary or compatible considerations: legal protection of human beings and their rights on the one hand and physical violence which endangers human beings and undermine their rights on the other.

The history of war is as old as the history of man. Throughout this history, however, a number of factors have made themselves felt, and have in varying degrees made for restraint in armed strife. These factors are at the root of humanitarian law, and led to its emergence and development by motivating parties to observe it. In fact, apart from the general (and formal) factor of the weight of legal obligation, the observance of humanitarian norms depends on the motivations of the parties to the conflict and on the role third parties can play to enhance such observance. What are these motivations which militate in favour of humanitarian norms and their observance?

1. **Moral imperatives**: religions as well as ancient civilizations provide us with multiple examples of certain codes of ethics ordering moderation and humane concern for the enemy in armed conflict, in the same way as the traditions of chivalry in the Middle Ages in Europe. These moral imperatives constitute internal, subjective and unilateral motivations and do not depend on the behaviour of the enemy. Indeed, in many cases, they tend to

demonstrate the moral superiority of those who follow them over their adversaries.

2. **Self-interest**: calculation is part of all wars. From the time prisoners, instead of being killed, were used as a source of man-power, as slaves, to the more subtle considerations of psychological warfare, of trying to turn around the enemy population through restraint and humane gestures, the calculated self-interest of the belligerents had led in many situations to a posture of self-limitation. Self-interest can also be a corporate or class interest of mercenaries or professional soldiers, for example, in order to minimize unnecessary harm and to maintain discipline. Self-interest is a unilateral motivation, based on objective calculation.

3. **Mutual interest**: here an element of reciprocity may lead the parties to mutual restraint, for example in the treatment and even-tually the exchange of prisoners, as well as in the treatment of enemy civilians. The motivation of each party is to some extent a function of the behaviour of the other; and there is an assump-tion that both belligerents are roughly in similar or comparable posi-tions (not necessarily in actual fact, but in general over a long period and a large number of armed conflicts).

4. **Community interest**: restraints may be prescribed in defence of higher values, i.e. of the values of a large community which encompasses but goes beyond the belligerents, e.g. historically, the *Res publica christiana* or the *jus cogens* norms of contemporary international law.

These factors are of course different in their rationale and con-sequently in the way they bear on the behaviour of the belligerents. Their differences determine also the role that third parties can play in enhancing the observance of humanitarian norms.

It is principally in relation to humanitarian norms based on the last two motivations, i.e. mutual interest and community interest, that third parties can play a useful role. But this role can differ in the two cases. While in the former their role is basically that of an intermediary or a go-between, in the latter case they can also speak in the name of the community as a whole in requesting the parties to conform to the restraining norms.

To what extent and in what ways, if any, have these factors and motivations been taken into consideration and built upon in the succession of legal instruments which have been adopted since the second half of the 19th century and which purport to codify and develop 'the law of war'?

I—The early evolution of international humanitarian regulation

The history of the advent and evolution of conventional humanitarian norms since the middle of the 19th century up to the present has been the history of the evolving balance between 'military necessities' and the 'requirements of humanity'. These are, however, highly evolving factors (one being objective, depending on the evolution of military technology and strategic thought; the other subjective, depending on the evolving perception and moral reaction of man and of the international community, i.e. on its threshold of tolerance). And though the Declaration of St. Petersburg (1868) speaks of 'the technical limits at which necessities of war ought to yield to the requirements of humanity', in actual fact humanitarian norms and their development were accepted by States to the extent they did not alter or interfere with the military balance between the potential belligerent parties.

This explains why the ensuing legal regulation was strongly based on considerations of mutual interest and inexorably conditioned by reciprocity. Thus a prominent feature of the legal instruments adopted before the first World War was the so-called 'si omnes' clause, by virtue of which if one of the belligerents is not party to the legal instrument, the instrument does not apply at all in the armed conflict, even between the belligerents which are parties to it. This was obviously to avoid any distortion of the military balance or conceding an advantage to the non-party as a result of an application of the instrument to some of the belligerents only.

The type of legal regulation which these instruments used also reflected the spirit of the age, particularly as concerns the question of guarantees, or rather lack of them, for their observance.

Indeed, these instruments partake of the general weakness of all international law, namely, the lack of central organs which can ultimately proceed to an authoritative interpretation of the norms and the determination of violations and their eventual sanction. Thus, in the great majority of cases (that is, unless such procedures and mechanisms are provided for or established in the treaty itself or in another instrument), the final guarantee for the proper discharge of their obligations remains the good faith of the parties and the factual considerations of reciprocity as well as, in certain cases, the varying weight of support or reprobation of public opinion.

But humanitarian law instruments, unlike those of the law of peace, suffer from a considerable additional handicap. For good faith (and its perception or expectation by the other party, i.e. mutual confidence) can hardly be assumed in the psychological atmosphere and under the stress of war, which are precisely the conditions in which humanitarian norms are called upon to apply.

Similar problems attend the sanction of violations. The classical sanctions of international law yield extremely counter-productive results in the context of humanitarian law instruments. *Durante bello*, the only sanction which was available to the aggrieved party was the negative version of reciprocity, i.e. reprisals in kind by not observing the norm violated by the other belligerent, or indeed any other norm of the instrument, or even the instrument as a whole. In other words, reprisals lead to the erosion of the standards and values for whose safeguard these instruments were adopted and which constitute their very object and purpose. *Post bellum*, there was not much that could be done beyond exacting compensation, a sanction which had no real deterrent effect, particularly since it always took the form of victor's justice by being inflicted only upon the defeated party.

Given the legal structure of these instruments, they obviously did not provide any role for third parties. Even the early Geneva Conventions, though they provided for the care of the wounded and sick in the battlefield and for the immunity of medical and relief personnel, did not provide any explicit legal basis for an independent role for the International Committee of the Red Cross (ICRC). The role of the ICRC did grow in practice, however, as a centre for information and relief.

It was during the First World War that the Hague Regulations of 1907, particularly their provisions concerning prisoners of war, came to be applied. The Hague Regulations and the Conventions to which they were appended did not provide for any special mechanisms for implementation, which were thus left entirely to the parties. But two factors came to modify this situation. In the first place, the parties to the conflict appointed Protecting Powers, a venerable diplomatic institution, to secure the representation and protection of their interests vis-à-vis those States with whom they were at war. The Protecting Powers considered it a matter of course to see to it that the obligations ensuing from the Hague Regulations and owed to the States they represented were also respected. Accordingly they made representations in this sense when the need arose and undertook visits to prisoners of war for that purpose. Similarly, the ICRC which had established in practice its right to send relief to war victims, by providing it directly to them, thus found itself present in prisoners of war camps, and undertook as a matter of course to comment to the detaining power on the conditions of those prisoners in the light of the Hague Regulations.

The experiences of the First World War fostered the new framework for the implementation of humanitarian norms called 'control' (changed to 'scrutiny' in 1949). It was a preventive/corrective technique aimed at establishing an early warning system of potential violations. The third party, through periodic verifications, could draw the attention of the detaining power to situations where the treatment of the prisoners of war fell below the prescribed standards, or where certain developments threatened to reach that point, the purpose being to remedy such situations either by preventing the violations from taking place, or by putting an end to continuous violations. The great advantage of this technique was to play on the spiral of reciprocity in a positive rather than a negative sense, to incite the parties to behave better, leading to similar conduct from the other belligerent party.

The encouraging result of this new technique led to its codification in the 1929 Geneva Prisoners of War Convention, where both the role of the Protecting Powers and the ICRC were recognized. Article 86 of that Convention considers the institution of the Protecting Power as an additional 'guarantee' for the regular application of the Convention and casts its role basically in terms of its collaboration with the detaining power (as well as with the opposite Protecting Power of the opposite party) for the proper implementation of the Convention. In other words, it is anchored on the concept of the mutual interest of the belligerent parties in the proper implementation of the Convention all around.

The great consecration of the technique of scrutiny found its expression, however, in the 1949 Conventions.

II—The Geneva Conventions of 1949

1. The role of the Protecting Power

As with earlier Conventions, the provisions of those of 1949 are addressed in the first place to the Parties which are called upon to implement the obligations provided therein. In addition, and this is an innovation of these Conventions, the Parties are made 'their brothers' keepers' by article 1, paragraph 1, which provides 'The High Contracting Parties undertake to respect and to ensure respect for the present Convention in all circumstances'. But the centre-piece of the system of scrutiny in the 1949 Conventions is the institution of Protecting Power, which was given a much greater role than in 1929:

a) Its ambit was greatly extended from the Prisoners of War (now the third) Convention to the first two on the Wounded, Sick and Shipwrecked (which implies its presence and operation on the theatres of war) as well as the fourth Civilians Convention (extending its presence and activities to whole countries or occupied territories and their populations).

b) From being an optional guarantee, the institution of Protecting Powers became a central and mandatory part of the system of implementation of the Geneva Conventions. Common article 8/8/8/9, paragraph 1, makes this abundantly clear when it provides that the Conventions 'shall be applied with the co-operation and under the scrutiny of the Protecting Powers.' This wording reflects an intention to consider the Protecting Powers not simply as representatives or mandatories of the parties to the conflict but also as organs of the Conventions and of the conventional community as a whole, i.e. as guardians of the community interest.

Yet, if the language of the first paragraph of common article 8 implies that the institution is mandatory under the Convention, the activation of the institution still remains in the hands of the parties to the conflict and the States which would act as their Protecting Powers. Thus, the appointment of a Protecting Power implies a triangular relationship requiring the consent of the power of origin, of the Protecting Power and of the detaining power. The withholding of its consent by any of these three States would prevent the institution from functioning.

c) The functions of the Protecting Power under the Conventions have both been spelt out in more detail and made all-pervading, covering all aspects of the application of the Conventions. Though they vary with the Conventions they can be classified into three categories:

i)   liaison functions between the detaining power, the protected persons and the power of origin;

ii) relief activities in favour of protected persons;

iii) scrutiny of the implementation of the Conventions by the detaining power, particularly in its treatment of the protected persons, to make sure of its conformity with their rights under the Conventions.

d) The great importance attributed to the institution by the Conventions is also revealed by their concern to provide, in common article 10/10/10/11, for a whole series of substitutes in case of absence of a Protecting Power, including, if all else fails (i.e. a substitute organization, or a substitute State appointed by the detaining power), paragraph 3 which provides that '. . . the Detaining Power shall request or shall accept [which means it is legally bound to accept] . . . the offer of services of a humanitarian organization such as the ICRC to assume the humanitarian functions of the Protecting Powers under the Conventions.'

Paradoxically, however, the institution of Protecting Power which proved its usefulness and vigour before it was largely codified in the Conventions, all but ceased to function since its adoption. Indeed, since then it was resorted to only four times (Suez 1956, Goa 1961, the Indo-Pakistani war of 1971 and the Falklands-Malvinas, 1982); and even then its functioning was fortuitous, incomplete or controversial.

The assumption which prevailed during the elaboration of the Conventions that States would never hesitate to appoint and accept, or to serve as, Protecting Powers was thus disproved in practice. The default of the institution was not so much the result of a 'non-possumus' (the assumption underlying the substitute system in common article 10/10/10/11) but of a 'non-volumus'. Several considerations were put forward to explain this lack of political will, which can be briefly summarized as follows:

i) If one of the parties to the conflict did not recognize the other, it hesitated to appoint a Protecting Power or to accept the appointment of one by its adversary, lest this would be interpreted as amounting to recognition, especially in view of the diplomatic origins of the institution (e.g. the Middle East).

ii) In certain cases, the parties continued to maintain their diplomatic relations in spite of the hostilities. This gave the detaining or occupying power an excuse for refusing the appointment of a Protecting Power, as long as the power of origin was directly represented, while at the same time denying the diplomatic representatives of the latter the possibility of exercising the functions of the Protecting Power under the Conventions (Sino-Indian conflict, 1962; Indo-Pakistani war of 1965).

iii) In view of the prohibition of the threat or use of force by the United Nations Charter, in some cases, though engaged in hostilities, the parties may be reluctant to admit the existence of an armed conflict between them.

iv) The procedure of appointment of Protecting Powers is cumbersome and calls for negotiations and agreement between the belligerents in the heat of battle, which is not usually easy to achieve. Moreover, in contemporary armed conflicts, hostilities as such *are* often a matter of a few days. This makes it extremely improbable to reach an agreement between the belligerents before the end of hostilities. After that the problem becomes less urgent and more difficult to resolve in isolation from the other aspects of the conflict.

v) It is difficult to find suitable neutral States, able and willing to fulfil the functions of the Protecting Power. In the first place, although there has been no general conflagration, the cold war gave birth to alignments which radically reduced the number of States which could be accepted by the belligerents in a number of cases as really neutral (e.g. between the United States and North Vietnam). Moreover, in view of the extension of the role of Protecting Powers under the Conventions, States solicited to play this role may find the burden too demanding in terms of material and human resources, especially small States. Finally, possible political embarrassment vis-à-vis the detaining or occupying power may prove to be more determinant a consideration to some States than the service rendered to the ideals of the Conventions by assuming the role of Protecting Power.

vi) The extension of the role, functions and attributions of the Protecting Power may have rendered the institution too cumbersome for belligerent parties to accept submitting to its scrutiny willingly.

All these factors contributed to the paralysis of the institution, and *a fortiori* of the substitute provided. In the meantime, the gap had to be filled; and it was the ICRC which did so.

2. The role of the ICRC
The role of the ICRC has always developed in the direction of its increasing involvement in the relief and protection of war victims, independently from the legal instruments existing at the time. This trend is inherent in the humanitarian nature and functions of the ICRC and reflects what has come to be known as the 'right of initiative'. Thus common article 9/9/9/10 reserves to the ICRC (and in theory to other impartial humanitarian organizations) the right (or rather the possibility) to undertake activities both within and outside the scope of the Conventions as long as they fall within the humanitarian field and are carried out with the consent of the States concerned.

But in addition to this general authorization, the Conventions confer on the ICRC an important role in the implementation of the Conventions, parallel to that of the Protecting Powers and consisting of certain specific functions and powers which are basically related to the Third and Fourth Conventions. Among them, three are of fundamental importance:

a) Articles 126 of the Third Convention and 143 of the Fourth confer on the ICRC, independently from parallel rights of the Protecting Powers, the right to visit prisoners-of-war and protected civilian detainees. This right is mandatory on the detaining power and is fundamental for the proper application of the Conventions.
b) Another function conferred by the Conventions on the ICRC in all circumstances is in the field of relief (Article 125, para. 3, of the Third Convention and 142, para. 3 of the Fourth).
c) Finally, an autonomous role for the ICRC is recognized in article 123 of the Third Convention and in Article 140 of the Fourth in relation to the Central Information Agency (concerning the tracing, gathering and transmission of information about protected persons).

These functions are to be undertaken by the ICRC in all cases in the same way as the Protecting Powers are required to do by the Conventions. The role of the ICRC becomes even more important, however, in the absence of a Protecting Power, for in such cases the question arises as to whether the ICRC can or should play the role of substitute as well. In the 1949 Diplomatic Conference, many delegations mentioned the ICRC in this respect. But representatives of the ICRC made it clear that it could not act as a 'complete substitute', because of its limited resources and strictly humanitarian mandate.

However, in view of the extensive interpretation adopted by the ICRC of the 'humanitarian functions' which it could undertake as a 'humanitarian quasi-substitute', by virtue of Article 10/10/10/11, paragraph 3, the refusal of the ICRC to act under the first two paragraphs was of no serious consequence. Indeed the ICRC declared more than once its willingness, in case of absence of a Protecting Power (or a complete substitute) to assume their humanitarian functions. It interpreted these functions as being all the functions of the Protecting Powers under the Conventions (to the exclusion of those derived from customary law). Scrutiny of implementation naturally figured at the top of the list of these humanitarian functions, it being unseverable from the substantive provisions of protection of which it guarantees the implementation. The only reservation made by the ICRC in this respect is that not being a 'Power', i.e. a State, it can fulfil these functions only to the extent to which its limited resources permit.

This initial position of principle gave place, however, to a more pragmatic attitude in practice. For the ICRC has always preferred to base its activity on its 'right of initiative', which is conditioned by the consent of the parties, rather than invoke the element of obligatory automaticity built into common Article 10/10/10/11, paragraph 3, which would have exerted a much stronger legal pressure on the recalcitrant party.

The discretion of the ICRC and its preference for the role of mediator to that of investigator were strongly contested and gave rise to serious controversies during the Vietnam war and the Middle East conflict since 1967. Indeed, the Middle East conflict of 1967 marked a significant development in this field, namely the assertion of a UN interest in the 'respect of human rights in armed conflicts'. This interest manifested itself not only through the resolutions adopted by several organs demanding the proper application of the Geneva Conventions in that conflict, but more significantly in their assumption of a parallel role to that of the ICRC in overseeing the implementation of the Conventions as a whole. This role grew as it became apparent that certain functions deemed essential for the safeguard of human rights and the proper application of the Conventions remained unfulfilled. Hence several fact-finding missions and *ad hoc* organs were established to investigate alleged violations of the Conventions in occupied territories.

* * *

These developments in the practice relating to the implementation of the 1949 Conventions led to the following conclusions. The Conventions were adopted under the immediate impact of World War II. They were inspired to a remarkable degree by what was then perceived as the community interest in the protection of war victims (parallel to the emerging system of international protection of human rights within the United Nations), going beyond the individual mutual interest of the belligerent parties. This 'higher' concept is reflected in many provisions of the Conventions, and more particularly in:

a) common article 1: 'The High Contracting Parties undertake to respect and ensure respect for the present Convention in all circumstances' establishing the principle of the collective interest in, and responsibility of each and every party for, the respect of the norms in all situations;

b) the casting of the Protecting Powers in the role of organs or representatives not only of the power of origin but of the conventional community as a whole, and imparting them with an all-pervading role of co-operating in and particularly overseeing the proper implementation of the Conventions by the parties;

c) the legal obligation of the parties, in the absence of a Protecting Power, to accept the offer of a humanitarian organism, to assume the humanitarian functions of the Protecting Powers (which was understood by the ICRC as covering all these functions, including scrutiny) under the Conventions (common Article 10/10/10/11, para. 3).

Experience reveals that it was precisely the provisions inspired by this all-sweeping concept of community interest, which failed to be translated into reality. Practice stopped short at the level of norms and solutions based upon the personal or mutual interest of the belligerent parties.

III—The 1977 Additional Protocol

A major reason and focus of the recent drive for the reaffirmation and development of humanitarian law, culminating in the adoption in 1977 of two Protocols additional to the Geneva Conventions, was the relative ineffectiveness of the system of implementation and scrutiny provided by these Conventions. Most of the proposals made in this respect found their way in their original or modified form to article 5 of the First Protocol (dealing with international armed conflicts), and subsidiarily to two other articles, 7 and 90.

1. Article 5

Article 5 ('Appointment of Protecting Powers and their substitute') contains several non-controversial paragraphs such as 5 and 6, which provide assurances or clarifications designed to assuage some of the apprehensions which were assumed to be at the root of the reluctance of belligerents to appoint Protecting Powers. The former provides that such appointment does not affect the legal status of the parties or of any territory, including occupied territory; while the latter specifies that the maintenance of diplomatic relations or the resort to the representation of interests between the belligerents does not constitute an obstacle to the appointment of Protecting Powers. Similarly, paragraph 6 aims at facilitating the procedure of appointment by requesting the ICRC to take the initative of acting as an intermediary between the parties for that purpose.

These two sets of provisions aim at facilitating the process (both in terms of decision and procedure) of appointment of Protecting Powers, but not at guaranteeing the existence of a mechanism of protection in all circumstances. Proposals going beyond that inevitably turned around the idea of an international substitute, which would provide a safety net or fall-back solution in case of non-appointment of Protecting Powers. It was inevitable that the ICRC be considered as the most suitable substitute. The ICRC put forward two alternative proposals to that effect, which constituted a step forward in the attitude of the ICRC in comparison to 1949 in that they indicated a willingness on its part to act as a substitute in certain circumstances. However, both alternatives (as well as the final adopted version, paragraph 4 of article 5) remained resolutely consensual at both ends: the ICRC (or another humanitarian organization) can, but is not obliged to make an offer to act as a substitute of the Protecting Power; and the parties are not obliged to accept this offer if it were made. This provision was strongly criticized in the Diplomatic Conference as threatening to erode the measure of legal compulsion and automaticity which is built into common article 10/10/10/11, paragraph 3, of the Conventions, if the 1949 provisions are restrictively and retroactively interpreted in the light of those of the 1977 Protocol, which requires the consent of the parties to the functioning of substitutes without exception or qualification.

Be that as it may, paragraph 4 did not provide the safety net, the substitute of last resort, which would fill the gap in all circumstances. A last attempt to provide for an ultimate substitute to be established within the United Nations, designed to fill the gap or what would be left of it in case of inaction by the ICRC, was narrowly defeated in the Conference.

This led to the search of means of perfecting the system in other directions.

2. Article 90
Among the reasons given for the non-functioning of the institution of Protecting Power was the great extension of its role under the Conventions to the point of frightening eligible States from assuming such a charge. This also explains the reluctance of the ICRC to accept the role of a complete substitute, as it could not at one and the same time function as an intermediary depending on the good will of the detaining power and as a quasi-judicial instance investigating and reporting possible violations. Consequently attempts were made to separate these two functions and attribute the quasi-judicial function to another organ; whence the proposals for the creation of a fact-finding Commission (especially after the defeat of the proposals for an ultimate automatic substitute). But the final adopted text of article 90, watered down the proposal from a Commission with compulsory jurisdiction to a doubly consensual one, in the sense that it needs a separate accep-

tance of a certain number of States Parties to the Protocol to come into existence, and then yet another acceptance by the parties to a conflict to submit to its jurisdiction.

3. Article 7

Another potential means of scrutiny operating outside the consent of the parties was sought in the collective responsibility of the whole conventional community for the respect of the Conventions as enshrined in common Article 1. This was tried through an amendment to what has become Article 7 of the Protocol which provided for meetings of the Parties 'to consider general problems concerning the application of the Conventions and of the Protocol'; meetings which could have provided an institutional framework for collective scrutiny. But the amendment to delete the adjective 'general' before 'problems', thus extending the purview of these meetings to the examination of specific cases, was defeated (though a liberal interpretation of the text does not exclude such a possibility).

* * *

As regards the mechanisms of scrutiny with a view to ensuring the proper observance of humanitarian law, the 1977 Protocol has thus remained resolutely consensual. Each time the proposed improvements threatened to cross the Rubicon of the consent of States, the Diplomatic Conference held back.

This was the result of the strong inflexible position of the Socialist group in refuting any automatic mechanism or compulsory jurisdiction institution which rests exclusively on the Protocol and not on the concrete acceptance of the State concerned. In this they were followed by some, but by no means all or even the majority of Third World States, which, as the weaker members of the international community, are usually on the receiving end of the gravest violations of humanitarian norms, and thus have a strong interest in ensuring their proper observance.

The initial strong stand of Western States in favour of an effective system of scrutiny changed radically before the end of the exercise (with notable exceptions among the smaller States) into a complete endorsement of the socialist position. The formal argument for this radical change was the search for consensus, but probably it resulted from the declining US interest in the matter with the end of the Vietnam war, and even more so from the extension of the protection provided by the Protocol to means and methods of warfare (i.e. against the effects of bombardments).

As a result, the long and complex provisions of the Protocol in this regard represent marginal improvements over the Conventions rather than bold advances. Basically, they take the form of legal clarifications and assurances and procedural facilitating devices to incite States to act, as well as providing them with institutional mechanisms which they can use if they decide to act. But perhaps the total effect of these provisions is to ascribe to the ICRC an even greater role in this field. The Protocol provides it with solid and varied means of action. If the ICRC uses them from the beginning with daring imagination and firmness, the general context of the system of implementation and control of application of humanitarian law can be completely transformed. If on the other hand the attitude of the ICRC reflects too much hesitation or excessive prudence, as it sometimes did in the past, nothing would have been changed by the new texts, which are permissive (of ICRC action) rather than mandatory (for the Parties).

IV—Possible further action

The two Protocols additional to the Geneva Conventions were adopted in 1977 after almost ten years of laborious preparation and negotiations. It is too early now, and politically unfeasible, to embark on a new round of 'reaffirmation and development' of humanitarian law; the more so since Protocol I is criticized in some quarters as being too detailed and even militarily unworkable.

Six years after their adoption, the Protocols are ratified or acceded to by only a small fraction (about one fourth) of the States Parties to the Geneva Conventions. The first concrete action that should be undertaken with a view to enhancing observance of humanitarian law, is to undertake all the possible démarches, particularly through objective and respected bodies such as the Independent Commission, to persuade States of the usefulness and even the necessity of acceding to the Protocols. Beyond that, to have a chance of success, action has to be situated for the time being within the framework and the parameters of existing instruments rather than aim at modifying them.

Of the forces making for compliance with humanitarian norms, it is to the self-interest and mutual interest of the parties (hence reciprocity guaranteed by the requirement of consent) that the marginal improvements introduced by Protocol I have largely catered. This was done with the hope that they would induce the belligerent parties to make greater use of the mechanisms of implementation put at their disposal in the Conventions (particularly the institution of Protecting Power and its substitutes). It remains to be seen how effective these improvements will be in practice in achieving this aim. In terms of inducements for parties to act out of self- or mutual interest, there is little that can be added, beyond trying to demonstrate the existence of a mutual interest for both parties (hence an element of reciprocity) in the observance of certain norms in particular situations where the interest of one of the Parties is not discernible at first glance.

At the end of the spectrum, extreme sanctions, such as personal criminal responsibility for those who commit 'grave breaches' of humanitarian norms (a system introduced in the Geneva Conventions of 1949 in the wake of the Nuremberg and Tokyo trials, which assume at their basis a very strongly felt community interest), have yet to prove their effectiveness. Up to now, as with the classical sanction of compensation, they have been applied only *post bellum* and exclusively to the defeated party and its officials, which indicates that they have been used in the individual rather than the community interest. In any case, the system of 'grave breaches' has yet to receive practical application.

Between these two extremes (the purely consensual one based on self-interest and reciprocity, and formal sanctions), there is still room for some action aiming at reinforcing the respect for humanitarian norms within the parameters of existing legal instruments. As discussed below, such further action can take place both at the normative and the institutional levels.

1. Enhancing the visibility of humanitarian norms and of their violations

As was mentioned above, one of the main weaknesses of the present system of international law is the absence of mechanisms for the authoritative interpretation of its norms and determination of concrete instances of violations, apart from the further stage of sanctioning these violations. The particular system of scrutiny provided for in the Geneva Conventions has not functioned adequately, except for the intervention of the ICRC, which prefers to play a conciliatory role rather than 'find' or 'determine' and 'report' violations.

On the other hand, the Geneva Conventions and Protocols are lengthy, complex and intricate instruments, whose provisions leave much room for interpretation and argument with a view to escaping a clear-cut finding of a violation. Such rules do not easily lend themselves to the self-regulatory system of classical international law. Customary rules of international law have objective criteria for identifying the prescribed behaviour, and readily lend themselves to direct (and not easily contestable) determinations of violations by States, whether the parties or third States, in the absence of a centralized body of observations.

If the organic system of the Geneva Conventions has not functioned properly, the contents can be reformulated to adapt them better to the absence of this system; in other words, to reformulate them in such a way as to define very clearly in a simple, 'objective' and unqualified manner the prescribed behaviour and/or what would constitute a violation thereof. This would make humanitarian norms and their contents more easily accessible (and understandable) to those who are called upon to observe them, i.e. rank and file soldiers and officers, and thus contribute in no small measure to a wider and better observance of their prescriptions.

It would also enhance the visibility of the norms and of their violations, which can thus be directly observed by all members of the international community, without leaving much room for 'specious' argumentation by the faulty party on the basis of the qualification or the 'subjective' formulation of the norm.

This 'simplification' of the norms increases the role and the pressures of the international community, making for the observance of humanitarian norms, and thus the possibility of highlighting to a greater extent the community interest in such an observance.

Technically speaking, this 'simplification' of humanitarian norms does not necessarily call for a formal revision of the Conventions and their additional Protocols. It can be undertaken either privately through the preparation of a restatement of the basic principles and norms of humanitarian law, perhaps by a group of experts, under the auspices of the ICRC or the Independent Commission. Better still, either this restatement or another prepared initially by a Special Committee appointed for that purpose could be adopted as a Declaration by the UN General Assembly, which would give it more weight.

The preparation of such a simplified restatement raises another question. As was mentioned above, the existing legal instruments are too long, complex and intricate. It is generally considered that all their provisions are of a humanitarian nature and have *jus cogens* character. Yet it is equally clear that many of these provisions deal with operational details while others lay down basic principles or fundamental prescriptions. In a way the abundance of the former tends to reduce the visibility, hence the impact, of the latter, and give a diluted impression of the whole.

The preparation of a simplified restatement would require a discriminating distinction between these two types of provisions to reformulate and include in it only the latter category; emphasizing the continued legal validity and force of the former, but merely as necessary technical annexes or appendices to the latter.

2. Fragmenting the functions of the Protecting Power and multiplying the substitutes

Work on the normative level in order to compensate for the deficiency of institutional mechanisms should not discourage attempts at remedying these deficiencies. Here again without resorting to formal 'revision' of the Conventions and the Protocols, there is still some room to build on certain legal potentialities which exist therein, but which have yet to be tried.

It is clear from all preceding analyses that the main weakness of all mechanisms of scrutiny lies in their exclusively consensual basis. This is true of the institution of Protecting Power under the Conventions, as well as of the role of the ICRC as a substitute under Protocol I (Article 5/4) and the International fact-finding Commission (Article 90). However, there is a legal way of qualifying this consensual basis, not by by-passing it but by tracing it back to the Conventions themselves. Indeed, as was mentioned above, common Article 10/10/10/11, paragraph 3, provides a measure of legal compulsion, by making obligatory on States parties the acceptance of the offer of a humanitarian organization to fulfil the humanitarian functions of the Protecting Powers. As was also mentioned above, the ICRC interpreted these functions as all the functions of the Protecting Powers under the Conventions, including scrutiny. But in practice, the ICRC has rarely, if ever, invoked this article, preferring to act on the basis of its right of initiative which is subject to the consent of States. This preference reflects the conviction of the ICRC that there may be a tension and even a contradiction between its conciliatory role as an intermediary aiming first and foremost at providing assistance and relief to war victims, a role which depends very much on the goodwill of the detaining power, and the role of supervisor that scrutiny implies, which requires verification and taking position on allegations of violations. And it is not certain that Article 5/4 of Protocol I will deflect this attitude.

Common Article 10/10/10/11, paragraph 3, is not limited to the ICRC, however. Thus in case of absence of Protecting Powers, and the non-fulfilment of all or part of their humanitarian functions, including scrutiny by the ICRC, common Article 10/10/10/11, paragraph 3, provides an unimpeachable legal title or 'locus standi' for action by any humanitarian organization which would be willing to fill the gap. And the detaining or occupying power is legally bound to accept the offer of such an organization, once it is made.

Of course, as with any legal obligation, the detaining power may refuse to honour it and permit the organization to function. But this attitude in itself would constitute a flagrant breach of common Article 10/10/10/11, paragraph 3, of the Conventions and would create a presumption against the proper discharge of its obligations under the Conventions and Protocol by the refusing State.

The humanitarian organization can be an existing body within or without the UN system (such as the Independent Commission), or an organ to be created specifically for that purpose (by the General Assembly, the Human Rights Commission, etc.).

This was tried by the UN in the aftermath of the Middle East conflict of 1977, but the results of this experience were not conclusive owing to the refusal of the occupying power to cooperate with UN fact-finding organs and to permit them to visit the occupied territories. The lesson to be drawn from this and similar experiences in the field of human rights is that an organ created especially to investigate a particular situation is likely to be more suspect in the eyes of the concerned States than a standing organ which existed before the occasion for the investigation arises.

It is probably in relation to the scrutiny function that the danger of a vacuum exists, since it is likely that the ICRC would usually fulfil the other functions of the Protecting Power, if it is absent. The existence (or establishment) of a standing humanitarian organism to undertake this function on the basis of common Article 10/10/10/11, paragraph 3, would help greatly in filling this vacuum. This would lead to the fragmentation of the functions of the Protecting Power in its absence, and their assumption by more than one humanitarian substitute. On the one hand, the ICRC would continue to play the pragmatic role of the intermediary, trying to avoid taking positions and concentrating on practical measures in favour of the protected persons, to the extent the circumstances and the good will of the detaining power permit. On the other hand, the fact-finding component of the scrutiny function can be assumed by another, preferably standing, humanitarian body whether within or outside the UN.

In relation to fact-finding (apart from its facilitation through the simplification and greater visibility of the norms and of what constitutes a violation) a useful practical development would be to encourage NGOs to play a greater role in providing information (as they do in the field of human rights).

3. Activating the collective responsibility of the Parties in the proper observance of the Conventions and the Protocols

As has been said earlier, enhancing the visibility of the humanitarian norms and of their violations would make it easier for all members of the international community to observe or 'determine' violations directly. This task would be further facilitated by the work of fact-finding bodies, basing themselves on common Article 10/10/10/11, paragraph 3. But the determination of violations is not an end in itself, nor the end of what can be done. A firm legal basis for collective as well as individual stands and representations (démarches) by all Parties to the Conventions, (i.e. members of the conventional community, which in this case is almost coextensive with the international community) can be found in common Article 1 of the Conventions which provides: 'The High Contracting Parties undertake to respect and to ensure respect for the present Convention in all circumstances'. But neither the Conventions nor the Protocols indicate how to give effect, in practice, to this collective responsibility, the responsibility of upholding the community interest in the proper observance of their prescriptions.

The discharge of responsibility can take place through individual representations as well as collective action by the Parties within pre-existing fora such as those of the UN or the International Red Cross Conferences. But it can also be exercised within a Conference of the Parties, as provided for in Article 7 of Protocol I. This does not preclude the examination of specific cases, as 'the general problems of the application of the Conventions and the Protocol' can arise in relation to (or can be illustrated by) a specific case.

In any case, whatever the interpretation given to Article 7 of Protocol I, common Article 1 of the Conventions provides the Parties with an unimpeachable legal basis for a collective examination, in whatever form, including a Conference especially convened for that purpose, of cases of flagrant violations of the humanitarian principles and norms enshrined in the Conventions and further specified in the Protocols.

V—Wars of national liberation

Legally speaking, wars of national liberation constitute a species of international armed conflicts. Article 1, paragraph 4, of Protocol I provides:

> The situations referred to in the preceding paragraph [i.e. international armed conflicts] include armed conflicts in which peoples are fighting against colonial domination and alien occupation and against racist régimes in the exercise of their right of self-determination, as enshrined in the Charter of the United Nations and the Declaration on Principles of International Law concerning Friendly Relations and Co-operation among States in accordance with the Charter of the United Nations.

As such, all that has been said concerning the observance of humanitarian norms in international armed conflicts integrally applies to wars of national liberation.

These wars, however, raise certain particular problems which need to be specifically taken into consideration. Wars of national liberation are, at least in their early stages, 'asymmetric conflicts'. These are conflicts between radically unequal parties in terms of the resources they command, especially fire-power, mastery of the air and technological know-how in general. Liberation movements have to resort to unconventional or guerrilla warfare, if they want to survive and continue the struggle. But this type of warfare fits badly into the pattern of the Geneva Conventions which were cast in the mould of conventional warfare. However, neither asymmetry nor guerrilla warfare are limited to wars of national liberation. One can find them in many inter state wars. One of the main merits of the 1977 Protocols is the effort they reflect to adjust humanitarian law to the specific conditions of guerrilla warfare (including wars of national liberation).

It is true that the practical implementation of some provisions of the Conventions and the Protocol pose very serious problems to liberation movements. But these problems are not insurmountable. For example, there have been several recent cases of exchange or repatriation of prisoners of war held by liberation movements, and the treatment of such prisoners, given the circumstances of liberation movements, does not compare unfavourably with that practised by their adversaries, or by detaining States in general.

For as was eloquently said by the representative of Frelimo in the Diplomatic Conference, [the] essential requirement . . . [is] not the technical apparatus or the material means, but the will to apply the principles of humanitarian law.

In these circumstances, even if some technical requirements of the Conventions are impossible to satisfy, owing to the conditions of guerrilla warfare or the absence of a State structure, these would usually relate to the modalities of implementation rather than to the essence of the rules. With goodwill, an equivalent modality of implementation, feasible in the conditions of liberation movements, which corresponds to the essence, if not exactly to the letter, of the rule, can always be found.

The problem does not reside then in the inability of, or impossibility for, liberation movements to discharge their obligations under the Conventions and the Protocol. It resides in the radical negation of their existence by their adversaries. It is more than probable that governmments falling into one of the three categories enumerated in Article 1, paragraph 4, will never ratify or accede to the Protocol. But this does not mean the end of all hope of bringing humanitarian law to bear on wars of national liberation.

Indeed, most of the provisions of Protocol I (and not only those relating to wars of national liberation), follow a general and consistent pattern evident in the successive instruments of humanitarian law: they clarify the solution of issues which proved to be controversial under the Geneva Conventions or elaborate in greater detail, and in the light of experience, certain pre-existing general rules, whence the double denomination 'reaffirmation and development'.

The controversy over the international status of wars of national liberation arose in relation to the Geneva Conventions. Article 1, paragraph 4 of the Protocol clearly reveals the general consensus on the proper solution to be given to this problem, while indicating at the same time the interpretation that should prevail under the Geneva Conventions. Thus, the significance of the Protocol as the proper interpretation of the Geneva Conventions in their application to contemporary armed conflicts, an interpretation which is subscribed to by a very large majority of the parties to these Conventions, cannot be over-estimated.

Even if Protocol I is not accepted as a separate legal instrument by the handful of governments facing a war of national liberation, its provisions assert themselves as the proper interpretation of the Geneva Conventions. In this respect, the fact that the *locus standi* of liberation movements was codified in Article 96, paragraph 3, vindicates earlier interpretations of the term 'Power' in the Conventions to include such movements, at least for the purpose of common Article 2, paragraph 3 of the Conventions, whose formula was more or less borrowed by Article 96 of the Protocol.

This means that if a liberation movement makes a declaration accepting the provisions of the Conventions, according to common Article 2, paragraph 3, these Conventions, as interpreted in the light of Protocol I, become applicable in the on-going war of national liberation, regardless of the opposition of the adversary government, as long as it is itself bound by the Conventions.

It could still be argued that notwithstanding the declarations of the liberation movements and the legal arguments that one can put forward as to their effect, the application of the Conventions and the Protocol in wars of national liberation remains a moot question, because the adversary governments shall never accept or admit such a possibility. This attitude is not improbable; but it would constitute a violation of the Conventions. Unfortunately, violations of humanitarian law in general are not infrequent, being, as it is, called upon to apply in the psychological atmosphere and under the stress of war.

However, even wars of national liberation are not completely devoid of forces making for compliance with humanitarian law. Moreover, from a purely practical point of view, the adversary governments should have an interest in directing the liberation movements towards a law-abiding, hence a more predictable, attitude; and failing that (if the liberation movements do not honour their obligations under the Conventions and the Protocol) in exposing their lawlessness. Liberation movements for their part, given their inadequate resources and the vulnerability of the civilian population for whose sake they are fighting, have a strong interest in humanitarian law.

It is true that the asymmetrical character of wars of national liberation (at least in the beginning) may lead some to conclude that reciprocity is absent in such wars because reprisals in kind such as mass bombardments or mass arrests are not within the reach of liberation movements; but in fact they can react and inflict harm on their adversary in other ways. Hence a certain level of reciprocity exists all the same.

Be that as it may, the often heard opinion that reciprocity (or to look at its other, ugly, face—reprisals) is the ultimate and strongest factual guarantee for compliance with the law in armed conflicts, is rather simplistic. For, with the exception of total war between the greatest and the mightiest—what can be called the war of Titans—reciprocity (or reprisals) is never the only sanction, nor in many cases the most important one. It blends in varying ways and degrees with the other forces which favour compliance with humanitarian law. These forces differ according to the type and circumstances of each armed conflict.

This is because, unlike the wars of the Titans, these conflicts take place within the international community, not above or beside it. Parties have to contend with the attitudes and reactions of third parties and of the international community as a whole, which can determine, sometimes to no small extent, the very outcome of the conflict. In humanitarian law, this reaction is institutionalized and given a legal basis in common article 1 of the Conventions, as we have just seen.

If a war of national liberation breaks out, this legal basis enables the ICRC, international organizations and third States, as a minimum, to act on the assumption that the Conventions, as interpreted by the Protocol, are applicable to this war, to deal with the liberation movement and to demand and work for the protection of the victims on that basis. It is by increasing the cost or the nuisance value of non-compliance, that the international community can influence, and eventually transform, the attitude of the reluctant party.

Respect of Humanitatian Norms in Non-International Armed Conflict

Antonio Cassese

Contents

Antonio Cassese is Professor of International Law, University of Florence. He was member of the Italian delegation at the Diplomatic Conference on the Reaffirmation and Development of International Humanitarian Law Applicable in Armed Conflicts (1974-77); member and elected Rapporteur of the United Nations Sub-Commission on Prevention of Discrimination and Protection of Minorities (1977). Editor of 'New Humanitarian Law of Armed Conflict' (1979); author of several studies in the field of humanitarian law and human rights, notably 'Means of Warfare: the traditional and the new law' (1979); 'Current Trends in the Development of the Law of Armed Conflict' (1974).

I The General Background

The whole approach of international law to civil strife rests on an inherent clash of interests between the 'lawful' Government on the one side (which is of course interested in regarding insurgents as mere bandits devoid of any international status and subject solely to its own domestic criminal law) and rebels on the other (naturally eager to be internationally legitimized and considered internationally legal persons). Third States may, and actually do, side with either party, according to their own political or ideological leanings, and this of course further complicates the question.

Another important feature of the whole corpus of rules concerning internal armed conflicts should be stressed. The bulk of these rules has an exclusively humanitarian scope and purpose. It aims at protecting all civilians who do not take part in hostilities and may directly or indirectly suffer from armed violence, or the wounded and sick who, having taken part in armed violence, are no longer in a position to fight. Methods of combat are not regulated, except to the extent that this serves to spare civilians; in practice, no rule places restraints on the actual fighting of Government authorities and rebels '*inter se*' (there is only one minor exception: Article 4.1 in fine of Protocol II of 1977, in which 'to order that there shall be no survivors' is prohibited). In short, States have decided to place no restrictions whatsoever on fighting, on the clear assumption that, being militarily stronger than insurgents, they may quell rebellion more easily by remaining untrammelled by law. This concept is proving increasingly fallacious, for at present rebels are assisted in various ways, especially militarily, by third States, and armed violence therefore is perpetrated with ferocious intensity and cruelty on both sides.

A third general element should be borne in mind. At present, civil wars increasingly break out in Third World countries. The historical and political reasons for this being so are well known and it is therefore not necessary to dwell on the matter. What is instead worth emphasizing is that mostly it is developing countries which have opposed attempts to expand the humanitarian rules on the matter, on the false assumption that such expansion might unduly enhance the role of rebels and, by the same token, restrain their own sovereign authority.

This idiosyncratic feature of current internal strife entails that when discussing the possible means of ameliorating the international legislation on the matter, one should always bear in mind the locus where such legislation is to be applied as well as the general attitude of the States more directly concerned by civil wars. This is why in the present paper, the discussion of the possible improvement of humanitarian law will be primarily geared to developing countries.

II Main Problems Concerning the Application of Humanitarian Law to Internal Armed Conflict

The foregoing considerations are intended to provide a general backdrop against which the specific problems concerning the application of the international regulation of civil commotion should be examined. In a nutshell, the following problems stand out.

Firstly, it is general knowledge that Article 3 common to the four Geneva Conventions of 1949 is not sufficiently applied in practice, although it has undoubtedly turned, it is submitted, into a rule of customary international law. Often States pay lip service to the humanitarian demands laid down in that all-important norm, but when it comes to the crunch, they either behave as if it did not exist at all or claim that the civil strife going on within their territory, being simply a minor domestic disorder, does not come within the purview of Article 3. Even States more prone to heed humanitarian demands show a marked recalcitrance at putting Article 3 into practice.

Secondly, Protocol II of 1977, after being widely resisted by developing countries at the Geneva Diplomatic Conference and severely mutilated before its adoption, has been ratified by a relatively limited number of States (only 52 compared with 59 that have ratified Protocol I to date[1] and the ratification process is not proceeding as quickly as one would have expected. This is very regrettable, for, in spite of all its defects and lacunae, it is important in that it broadens the humanitarian protection afforded to the victims of civil strife.

Thirdly, normally in case of internal armed conflict, States parties to the four Geneva Conventions of 1949 do not avail themselves of the fundamental right they have to demand that the State where civil strife is in progress comply with Article 3. It may be recalled that Article 1 common to the four Conventions stipulates that 'The High Contracting Parties undertake to respect and to ensure respect for the present Convention in all circumstances. It follows that any contracting party has the right as well as the duty to exact from any other party to respect among other things Article 3. Yet, in actual practice very few States have so far taken advantage of this rule (the rule has however been relied upon in a number of instances by UN bodies, particularly the General Assembly and the Commission on Human Rights).

A fourth drawback to the existing situation is that sometimes the ICRC, to which credit must be given for fulfilling humanitarian tasks of immense value, is hampered in its action by several impediments. A number of Third World countries feel that the ICRC is essentially a Western institution, for it consists only of Swiss nationals and unwittingly tends to propound a substantially Western outlook; they therefore endeavour to restrain its action as much as possible. Furthermore, the policy and method of work the ICRC has chosen, i.e. confidentiality, although it is admittedly very effective and accounts for the undeniable success of the ICRC in so many instances, proves to be scarcely beneficial in other instances—which are becoming more and more numerous. The ICRC, it is submitted, sometimes underrates the importance of the 'mobilization of shame'—at least as far as internal armed conflicts are concerned. To give just one illustration taken from a collateral field, that of human rights, it has been contended, and rightly so, that Uruguay, a country that has been for some years now under constant strictures by the UN Human Rights Committee for its gross violations of human rights, has not dared to withdraw its acceptance of the Optional Protocol to the Covenant on Civil and Political Rights of 1966. This is because Uruguay prefers to be the target of individual complaints and the consequent criticism by the Committee than become the subject of public condemnation in the UN General Assembly. A body of experts whose 'views' on violations of human rights have a relatively minor weight (even though they are made public), are less feared than a political body which has a formidable weapon at its disposal, namely resort to world public opinion by pointing out the misbehaving States to universal opprobrium.

A further flaw of the ICRC action is that on account of its policy of self-restraint and of its emphasis on concrete help to the victims of armed conflict, it tends to shun formal communications indicating to States what set of international rules are applicable to specific conflicts, namely whether such conflicts are covered by common Article 3, or come within the purview of Protocol II, or fall under the whole of the four Geneva Conventions and Protocol I. The failure to pronounce upon these legal issues entails not only that the State where the internal armed conflict is raging feels less constrained to stick to a specific set of international undertakings, but also that third States are less impelled to exact compliance with those rules from the State concerned. This point has been eloquently made by H.P. Gasser, Head of the Legal Division of the ICRC in a recent article, where, after noting that the ICRC is not vested with any quasi-judicial function and therefore has not to lay down the law, adds the following:

> 'Nevertheless, reality forces one conclusion upon us: if the ICRC has no clear and distinct attitude, then undoubtedly no stand will be taken on the obligations of the parties to the conflict under humanitarian law, and the victims of the conflicts will suffer most for the lack of such a posture. The statutory mandate of the ICRC to work for the faithful application of the Geneva Conventions is thus reinforced by a deficiency in the system for implementing the instruments of humanitarian law: the habit of parties to the Geneva Conventions who are not involved in a conflict to remain silent when humanitarian law is ignored. From this perspective, the ICRC has an obligation to speak out. The parties to the conflict need to be reminded of the law, so that they will respect it and so that the existence of this law will be affirmed and strengthened. Such action is intended to prevent the provisions of the Geneva Conventions and the additional Protocols from being forgotten.' [2]

III Suggestions for a More Satisfactory Implementation of Humanitarian Law

The foregoing considerations make it imperative to strengthen the present rickety framework of international legal regulation of domestic strife. As civil wars are a burning issue and States easily take offence at any attempt at extending or ameliorating international legal control of internal conflicts, the battle, as it were, should be fought on several fronts: a host of different devices will prove necessary for the purpose. Inevitably, some of them may turn out to be palliatives while others may turn out to be too daring.

1. Efforts at Wider Ratification of Protocol II

As stated above, notwithstanding all its defects, Protocol II should bind a far greater number of States. In particular, as civil strife increasingly besets developing countries, pressure to ratify it should be specifically put on them. Other groups of States should not, however, be neglected, if only because Western countries (except for Canada and the UK, which appeared rather lukewarm) and socialist countries repeatedly stated at the 1974-1977 Diplomatic Conference that they were favourable to any international instrument extending the protection of Article 3. it would indeed be contradictory first to support and press for the strengthening of an international treaty and then hold aloof, thereby contributing to its failure to take root in the world community.

For the purpose of prompting States to become parties to the Protocol, the Independent Commission on International Humanitarian Issues (henceforth: the Commission) might envisage the advisability of sending States a memorandum in which the importance of the Protocol is pointed out and, what is more important, the fact that it really does not constitute a 'major danger' for State sovereignty, for it is almost exclusively geared to protecting the victims of armed conflicts. This message should be conveyed to States in carefully worded language, and in particular the following elements should be highlighted:

a) The Protocol only covers large-scale armed conflicts, i.e. civil strife presenting all the characteristics of intensity, duration and magnitude of such conflicts as the Spanish and Nigerian civil wars. It does not apply to 'situations of internal disturbances and tensions, such as riots, isolated and sporadic acts of violence and other acts of a similar nature'. In fact, the progress made in 1977 turns out to be limited in two ways: first, on account of the paucity of the rules evolved; second, because they do not cover all classes of internal armed conflicts, but only those above a certain 'threshold'.

b) As pointed out above, the Protocol includes only humanitarian norms intended to protect civilians, the wounded, sick and shipwrecked, as well as those who are no longer taking part in the hostilities; it does not place restraints on the conduct of military operations as between the lawful Government and rebels (except for the norm prohibiting the declaration that no quarter will be given).

c) The Protocol does not grant rebels any international status whatsoever: like common Article 3, it advisedly refrains from legitimizing rebels internationally; the application of the Protocol cannot therefore entail the acquisition of an international standing by insurgents.

d) The Protocol does not grant rebels any status of privileged combatants; they remain subject to the criminal law of the State; the latter is therefore legitimized to treat them as common criminals punishable for the mere fact of taking up arms.

e) The Protocol explicitly enjoins third States not to meddle in any armed conflict raging on the territory of a State party. Article 3 indeed provides as follows:

> 1. Nothing in this Protocol shall be invoked for the purpose of affecting the sovereignty of a State or the responsibility of the Government, by all legitimate means, to maintain or re-establish law and order in the State or to defend the national unity and territorial integrity of the State.
>
> 2. Nothing in this Protocol shall be invoked as a justification for intervening, directly or indirectly, for any reason whatsoever, in the armed conflict or in the internal or external affairs of the High Contracting Party in the territory of which that conflict occurs.

This provision, included at the behest of developing countries, clearly stipulates that States are entitled to take all the requisite measures to put down rebellions breaking out on their territory, provided of course they remain within the humanitarian bounds set by Article 3 and the Protocol. Furthermore, it provides that third States should not take civil wars as a pretext for unduly interfering in the affairs of the Government involved in the conflict: the 'intervention' prohibited by the rule is clearly that of a third State which supports the rebels by direct or indirect means, or puts pressure on the lawful Government with a view to inducing it either to accept a given political or military solution or to discontinue requesting military help from other countries. In short, the rule intends to safeguard the sovereignty of the State concerned, by laying down that, within the limits set by the international humanitarian rules protecting the victims of the conflict, that State is at liberty to behave with all the latitude devolving upon it from its sovereign rights.

In short, the Commission should impress upon States that the Protocol merely aims at protecting civilians, children, women, the wounded, sick and shipwrecked, and that it does not go beyond this humanitarian purpose. What is more, the Commission should draw the attention of States to the fact that the persons just referred to are after all nationals of the State where the civil commotion is in progress and that similarly the works and installations, the cultural objects or places of worship that the Protocol protects are part and parcel of the national assets of the State, even though the civilians and the objects under the sway of the rebels are of course out of the control of the lawful Government. Thus, even if relations between the incumbent Government and insurgents are strained, to say the least, and each of them tends to consider the civilians under the control of the counterpart as 'enemies', in fact they belong to the same sovereign State; consequently, the cruelty attendant upon the conduct of war becomes all the more absurd and inhuman.

I should like to add that the fact that the memorandum at issue would be drawn up and circulated by the Commission could present a major advantage if for this purpose the Commission appoints a 'Comité de Sages' made up of three to five outstanding personalities from the Third World, and the memorandum formally emanates from them. Their authority and prestige, coupled with their being from precisely the area where civil strife is more likely to occur, might greatly enhance the chance of the memorandum being heeded by the States to which it should be addressed. By the same token, the Western and socialist countries to which the memorandum should also be sent, would find in the attitude and views of the 'Comité de Sages' a further spur to their becoming parties to the Protocol.

2. Adoption of Unilateral Declarations Laying Down an Undertaking to Abide by Basic Humanitarian Standards

The suggestion put forward above may not yield positive results, for States may still demur at the ratification of the Protocol lest it impose legally binding obligations considered too onerous. For this eventuality resort should be had to some flexible contrivance with a view to binding States, at least morally and politically, to observing the basic standards of humanitarian law. The forum where such standards should be laid down might be the UN General Assembly, which is the highest political forum in the world and the place likely to have considerable effect on public opinion at the political level.

Inspiration could be drawn from what has been done in the UN in the field of torture. It is well known that in 1977 the General Assembly, facing reports of the widespread use of torture in several States, adopted a resolution (32/64 of December 8, 1977,[3] by which it called upon member States to 'reinforce their support' of the UN Declaration on Torture and Other Cruel, Inhuman or Degrading Treatment or Punishment (res. 3452-X of December 9, 1975),[4] by making unilateral declarations along the lines of a text annexed to the resolution, and to deposit them with the UN Secretary-General; in addition, the General Assembly urged States to give 'maximum publicity' to their unilateral declarations and requested the Secretary-General to inform the General Assembly, in annual reports, of the unilateral declarations deposited by member States.

The resolution proved to be a notable achievement. A sizable number of States has thus far issued unilateral declarations (above forty) and the Secretary-General, in his annual reports, gives account of the increasing number of States heeding the exhortation of the General Assembly. The 'quality' of States is also indicative. Thus, one of the first States to make the declaration was Iran, during the period the Shah was still in power. A team of international experts appointed by the International Commission of Jurists went to Iran at the request of the Shah and actually determined that since the unilateral declaration had been issued the Shah had ordered the immediate discontinuance of torture by Savak, but nevertheless the sporadic practice of torture was still going on in spite of that order. This was reported to the Shah, who promised to see to it that his commands be carried out; however, he was then toppled, and a new regime took over. The whole story bears witness to the impact that the decision to issue the declaration had on the domestic situation in Iran and constitutes eloquent testimony of the importance of the device contrived by the General Assembly.

Taking the action of the General Assembly on torture as a model, the Commission could endeavour to urge States to pass a resolution at the General Assembly laying down the basic humanitarian principles by which every member State should abide in case of domestic disorder involving armed violence beyond sporadic and minor disturbances. The resolution should reformulate the standards laid down in common Article 3, the most important provisions of Protocol II, as well as the principles laid down in the General Assembly resolutions 2444-XXX of December 19 1968.[5] and 2675-XXV, adopted on December 9 1970,[6] (these resolutions cover any kind of armed conflict, including those international in character). The low threshold of common Article 3 should be examined and given more specific definition. Furthermore, to dispel possible fears of States, it should be stated in so many words that the observance of those humanitarian principles in no way entails the legitimation of rebels or the granting of international status to them, let alone the status of lawful combatants. A further important proviso of the resolution should be that its acceptance and the issuing of unilateral declarations would in no way detract from existing international instruments laying down legally binding rules. Member States should then be called upon to deposit with the UN Secretary General unilateral declarations by which they solemnly undertake to comply with those humanitarian principles in case of civil strife.

The system just propounded would have the following advantages:

a) the General Assembly resolution would reformulate in general terms the whole corpus of humanitarian standards applicable in time of civil strife, thus consolidating and amalgamating the principal existing rules, both customary and conventional;

b) by adopting a very low 'threshold' of application, it would avoid loopholes permitting States to claim that they are free to do what they please, for the domestic disorders occurring on their territory fall short of international standards;

c) in view of its non-binding character, it would enlist the support of a greater number of States than Protocol II;

d) the annual publication by the UN Secretary General of a report listing the States issuing the unilateral declaration would constitute a means of giving publicity to the undertakings of individual States;

e) in case of gross disregard of the principles embodied in the General Assembly resolution accepted by unilateral declarations, the General Assembly would be entitled at least to discuss the matter and to call upon the State concerned to stick to its moral and political undertakings; thus an important political forum would be made available for the purpose of inducing compliance with humanitarian law.

The suggestions just formulated could not be accused of weakening the existing international rules on humanitarian law, for, as pointed out above, it should be clearly specified in the General Assembly resolution that States issuing the unilateral declaration remain of course bound by their legal engagements: such declarations are not intended to replace but only to restate and reinforce those engagements for the States bound by them, while for the other States it would only be designed to elaborate upon and expand, albeit in non-binding legal terms, the international norms on civil war.

3. The Entrusting of Humanitarian and Supervisory Functions to a 'Comité de Sages'

I have already hinted at the advisability for the Commission to establish a 'Comité de Sages' consisting of prominent individuals of great prestige. The majority of the 'Comité' should be personalities from developing countries, and one may even wonder whether the whole 'Comité' should not be made up of individuals from those countries. This would ensure that the body were more acceptable to those Third World countries where civil wars happen to break out. To enable it to adapt itself flexibly to changing circumstances, it might consist of five persons, of different nationalities. The Chairman could appoint one to two or three of them for each armed conflict to be covered by the 'Comité'; the choice of persons should of course be dictated by considerations of nationality, etc. (thus, the normal rule should be that the persons in charge of a certain civil war should belong to the politico-geographic area where the conflict is raging).

The 'Comité' should primarily act under common Article 3: it is well known that para 2 of this provision stipulates that 'An impartial humanitarian body, such as the International Committee of the Red Cross, may offer its services to the Parties to the conflict'. Thus, the 'Comité' would perform the multifarious activities covered by the broad rubric of 'humanitarian services'. It could approach the Government where a domestic conflict is in progress and offer advice on the humanitarian rules applicable, or urge that Government to apply them. It could organize international relief operations for the victims of the conflict. It could endeavour to mediate between the contending parties in an effort to reach a political solution. It could monitor the observance of humanitarian law by the parties to the conflict. In sum, the 'Comité' could offer to fulfil all the various humanitarian and supervisory tasks normally devolving upon the ICRC, with the advantage of (i) being more acceptable to the incumbent Government (as well as, one may surmise, to the insurgents); (ii) being less hindered than the ICRC by internal regulations and practices, hence better able to adjust flexibly to the various circumstances, to the political context and the nature of the conflict; in a word, to be more supple than the ICRC. A further advantage of the setting up of the 'Comité de Sages' would be that the ICRC would be relieved of the burden of catering for all internal armed conflicts. One might envisage a sort of division of labour to the effect that the 'Comité de Sages' might decide to step in only when the various circumstances surrounding the armed conflict make it particularly inappropriate, or inadvisable, for the ICRC to intervene; in these instances the ICRC might confine itself to asking the 'Comité' to keep it informed of the turn of events and the evolution of its humanitarian mission.

4. The Determination by the 'Comité de Sages' of the Nature of the Internal Conflict and of International Humanitarian Standards Applicable

I have emphasized above that, on a number of grounds, including the need for pragmatism, the ICRC tends to gloss over the question of whether a given armed conflict is covered by common Article 3 or is instead governed by Protocol II or by the whole corpus of the 1949 Geneva Conventions and Protocol I. By contrast, the 'Comité' should envisage as one of its main functions the legal determination of the conflict and the establishment of the rules relevant to it. Resort to such determination should however constitute a fall-back solution: only if the State involved in the conflict refuses to co-operate with the 'Comité' and rebuffs its offer of good services, should the 'Comité' decide to make a formal and public statement on the legal nature of the conflict and the category under which it falls. The reason why such a step should be taken as a last resort is self-evident: States engaged in domestic strife prefer to keep things loose, and shun any definite legal classification so as to enjoy greater freedom of action. As long as they co-operate and are willing to accept the humanitarian and supervisory tasks of the 'Comité' this body should refrain from publicly making a finding on the matter. If however the Government concerned slams the door in the face of the 'Comité' or turns a deaf ear to its humanitarian appeals, there should be no room for hesitation.

The formal and public determination of the legal nature of the domestic war and the indication of the applicable rules have a twofold advantage. First, a prestigious and independent international body informs world public opinion that the civil commotion in progress in a given State exhibits certain features and that a certain set of international legal standards should be applied by the contending parties. This might result in strong pressure being exerted on those parties, particularly on the lawful Government, to the effect that they should comply with the relevant rules. The second and perhaps even more important advantage is that third States are implicitly called upon to face the situation squarely; in particular, they are *de facto* urged to take steps with a view to inducing the contending parties to abide by the relevant international rules. In case of continuing disregard of international humanitarian law by the parties to the conflict and of inaction on the part of third States, the 'Comité' could also take a further step and publicly remind those States of their right and duty, under Article 1 of the four Geneva Conventions of 1949, to demand compliance with at least common Article 3.

It stands to reason that the mere fact of vesting the 'Comité' with the authority to make the determination referred to, can prove instrumental in impelling Governments to cooperate with it: knowing that if they do not, the 'Comité' is empowered to make a formal and public pronouncement on the armed conflict, and that such a pronouncement may have so great an impact on world public opinion as well as on third States, that the Governments concerned may find it more expedient to allow the 'Comité' to exercise its humanitarian and supervisory tasks right from the beginning.

5. Fact-Finding by the 'Comité de Sages'

For the purpose of the present paper, it seems advisable to

distinguish between the 'supervisory' tasks of the 'Comité' and fact-finding properly so called. The former comprises routine monitoring of possible breaches of humanitarian law, by resort to the most varied means of scrutiny: reports of delegates of the 'Comité' who find themselves on the spot; reports by delegates of international institutions working in the area of conflict, or by national organizations of the country involved in the conflict, such as the Church, relief agencies, etc.; press reports, etc. By contrast, fact-finding implies a formal and quasi-judicial procedure of collecting evidence and assessing it against the relevant humanitarian standards; in addition, it is carried out with regard to specific instances of alleged violations of humanitarian law, hence not on a day-by-day basis. The following observations should be read in the light of this distinction.

It is well known that one of the crucial problems of internal strife is the determination of possible violations of the relevant international rules: appalling breaches occur very frequently, and usually it is civilians who suffer the most, but the contending parties normally deny their being involved in the perpetration of infringements, or else discount them, or even claim that the counterpart is answerable. It becomes therefore extremely important to establish where the truth lies and what can be done to avert the occurrence of atrocities in the future. It is common knowledge that Governments embroiled in civil strife rarely allow international organizations to conduct enquiries, and the same recalcitrance can be discerned in insurgents. It is also well known that the ICRC itself is somewhat reluctant to undertake on-the-spot investigations concerning means and methods of warfare and that, when it engages in fact-finding, on the strength of its international regulations and practices it usually refrains from making its findings public, but brings them to the knowledge of the parties concerned, with a strong appeal to discontinue violations as well as avoid similar or other breaches in future.

The 'Comité de Sages' could usefully undertake investigations into alleged violations of humanitarian law without being encumbered by the limitations affecting the action of the ICRC. In particular, it could rely more heavily on public opinion, by immediately disclosing its findings, and appealing to the parties concerned as well as to third States to do their utmost to avoid, or help to avoid, serious breaches.

On the operational level, the 'Comité' could carry out its enquiries with the help of its staff. If one of the contending parties refused to allow the fact-finding body into the area where the enquiry should be effected, the 'Comité' could publicize such a refusal and in addition endeavour to conduct the investigation all the same. This, it should be recalled, has happened several times within the UN, where member States (e.g. South Africa, Israel, Chile) have refused the international body of enquiry access to the place where the evidence was to be found. Those UN bodies have nevertheless carried out their investigation outside the territory of the State concerned, by collecting testimonials of exiles and refugees, documentary evidence, and so on. It goes without saying that in these cases the enquiry becomes much more difficult and the findings less unimpeachable. Nevertheless, the investigation could serve a useful purpose, by indicating to world public opinion on whom the blame for the failure to investigate the delinquencies should be placed. It could, in addition, provide at least circumstantial evidence concerning the breaches.

IV Concluding Remarks

By way of conclusion, it should be stressed that the bulk of the suggestions propounded above hinges on the concept that in a number of instances action by a prestigious and highly qualified body emanating from the Independent Commission on International Humanitarian Issues might fulfil the humanitarian and supervisory tasks that sometimes the ICRC cannot discharge for various reasons. The composition of the 'Comité de Sages', its flexibility of action, its being untrammelled by rules of confidentiality and self-restraint, its resort to world public opinion, might prove exceedingly useful at least in a number of cases. The action of the 'Comité' would thus not displace that of the ICRC, nor would it result in a regrettable overlapping. There might easily evolve a sort of division of labour between the two bodies, in view of their different composition, methods of work and available means. It goes without saying that the long experience of the ICRC, the wealth of financial means at its disposal as well as its having available a broad and solid network of well-trained and highly experienced delegates, are all elements that militate in favour of allotting to the ICRC a broader competence as regards domestic strife. The 'Comité de Sages' should therefore concentrate on the few instances of civil commotion, where the political and social context and the nature of the conflict make it particularly difficult for the ICRC to intervene effectively.

Whatever the division of labour to be established, it seems indisputable that both the ICRC and the 'Comité', if they decide to operate not on a competitive basis, but on a basis of helpful co-operation, might greatly contribute to mitigating the harmful effects of internal armed conflicts.

Notes

1. See Appendix I.
2. 'International—Non-International Armed Conflicts: Case Studies of Afghanistan, Kampuchea and Lebanon', in *The American University Law Review*, 1982, vol. 31, p. 924.
3. See Appendix IV.
4. See Appendix V.
5. See Appendix VI.
6. See Appendix VII.

Respect of Humanitarian Norms in Internal Disturbances and Tensions

Asbjørn Eide

Contents

Asbjørn Eide is former Executive Director, International Peace Research Institute, Oslo; former Secretary General, International Peace Research Association; former Member of the UN Sub-Commission on the Prevention of Discrimination and Protection of Minorities. He was a member of the Norwegian Delegation to the Diplomatic Conference on the Reaffirmation and Development of International Humanitarian Law. He is the author of several books and articles on human rights, peace-keeping and military issues.

I The problem and the need for new institutional solutions

Problems connected with internal disturbances and tensions are inadequately dealt with in contemporary international law and none of the established international agencies can deal properly with the concerns arising from these phenomena. There are embryonic developments which have taken place: one is the expanding role of the ICRC, seeking to extend its humanitarian initiatives to situations of internal disturbances and tensions; on the other hand, human rights organs of the United Nations are increasingly focusing on situations of gross and consistent violations of human rights. Internal disturbances and tensions very often give rise to such violations, and thus involve the human rights organs of the United Nations.

Despite these embryonic developments, it is unlikely that either the United Nations or the ICRC can deal adequately with this problem. They would have to go considerably beyond their primary orientation. Moreover, the problem of non-interference in domestic affairs of States seriously limits possible action by the United Nations.

There is a need, therefore, for new institutional solutions to develop the legal basis for meeting humanitarian concerns in situations of internal disturbances and tensions, and to promote and encourage compliance with these norms. In the evolution of norms, use can be made both of the body of humanitarian law and that of human rights. Adaptations will have to be made, however, to handle the special problems which arise in situations of internal disturbances and tensions.

1. The nature of the phenomenon

In its report entitled 'Protection of Victims of Non-International Armed Conflicts' presented to the first session of the Conference of Government Experts held in Geneva in 1971, the ICRC said that internal disturbances involve:

> ... situations in which there is no non-international armed conflict as such, but there exists a confrontation within the country, which is characterized by a certain seriousness or duration and which involves acts of violence. These latter can assume various forms, all the way from spontaneous generation of acts of revolt to the struggle between

more or less organized groups and the authorities in power. In these situations, which do not necessarily degenerate into open struggle, the authorities in power call upon extensive police forces, or even armed forces, to restore internal order.[1]

This description focuses on a confrontation between a government and a certain type of opponent. As will be shown below, this may be too limited an approach. The description refers also to the extensive use of police or even armed forces by the authorities. The ICRC had thus in mind conflict situations which have already escalated to a considerable degree, but which have not yet reached the level of 'armed conflict'. At this point, it should be recalled that Protocol II comes into operation only when the party opposing the government carries out armed action; and when that party consists of an organized armed force and controls a significant part of the territory. For the purposes of this paper, everything falling below this threshold is to be considered as coming under the label of 'disturbances and tensions', even if the government uses armed forces and even if the opposition does so too, as long as it does not control a significant part of the territory as foreseen in Article 1 of Protocol II.

In a subsequent document, the ICRC also referred to the concept of 'internal tension'.[2] 'Tension' can be defined as situations of a serious tenseness brought about by political, religious, racial, social or economic factors.

Let us therefore understand 'internal disturbances and tensions' as all situations of conflict inside a nation, serious enough to give rise to significant humanitarian concerns, in particular because it is leading to the use of physical violence and denials of freedom, whether or not organized armed force is used. The two most important categories are ethnic (and racial) conflicts, and social conflicts. In the former, two different populations oppose each other; in the latter, two different social groups oppose each other. Ethnic conflicts are often (though not always) a struggle for separation versus integration. Social conflicts, in their extreme, can be a question of revolution versus maintenance of the existing social order, or a counter-revolution seeking to re-establish the old régime.

Disturbances and tensions may be the beginning of revolutions or secessions. If this is the underlying nature of the conflict, the methods chosen to deal with these disturbances are of extreme importance, as will be discussed below.

Another category consists of conflicts brought about by discrimination, whether it be racial or religious. Unless the racially or religiously oppressed group is at the same time an ethnically coherent group, there is rarely a question of secession, or of revolution. When the different racial and religious groups are mixed within the same territory, the situation is less likely to result in organized armed action between groups. Nevertheless, the group which is discriminated against may be subjected to tremendous suffering, even to the extent of being eliminated.

One more category should be mentioned: protests by the young, which may be the result of frustration and deep dissatisfaction with the authorities, but which are neither a social revolt nor a racial or ethnic confrontation. This phenomenon has been observed in many Western countries in the last decade. On the fringe of such protests small but destructive terrorist groups have sometimes emerged. While their lack of social base has isolated them, they represent a challenge to the authorities which have responded by building up anti-terrorist forces. These, in turn, have sometimes given rise to human rights violations.

II The applicable norms

Two bodies of international law are relevant to these situations: humanitarian law and the international law of human rights. These two sets of laws have different origins and different concerns.

Humanitarian law is based on a set of rules derived from the 'Law of The Hague', which contains principles relevant to the rules of warfare, and the 'Law of Geneva', which contains in particular principles relevant to the protection of victims of armed conflict.

The fundamental principles of the laws of war (the law of The Hague) are to limit the means and methods of warfare, and to distinguish between combatants and non-combatants, in order to keep the latter group outside the field of operations; to limit legitimate targets to military objectives; and to prohibit the use of weapons and methods likely to cause unnecessary suffering. The basic principles of the Law of Geneva are concerned with the protection of the victims of armed conflicts, and the protection of persons who fall in the power of a party to the conflict. In other words, humanitarian law focuses on conflicts, or on situations of confrontation, between opposing parties or groups.

The international law of human rights is fundamentally different, in that it defines the rights of every human being. It is not concerned with situations of conflicts. This system is very comprehensive and consists of the following basic principles:

- self-determination of peoples (common Article 1 to the Covenants of 1966);
- fundamental freedoms, which include:
  * rights relating to the integrity of the individual,
  * freedom of action of the individual;
- political rights (the right to participate, to elect and be elected, together with other rights essential for such participation);
- social and economic rights (right to work, right to food, to education, etc.);
- cultural rights, which include:
  * the right to cultural identity and continuity (as provided in Article 27 of the International Covenant on Civil and Political Rights),
  * the right to participate in the cultural life of the society, and to enjoy the fruits of that activity.

In dealing with internal disturbances and tensions, we are faced with situations where there is some degree of conflict and confrontation, and where some of the problems occurring in armed conflicts also arise. The existing legal provisions have not been developed, however, with these situations in mind.

1. Common Article 3

By definition the provisions of Protocol II do not apply in times of internal disturbances and tensions. However, common Article 3 of the Geneva Conventions of 1949 may be applicable in some of these situations, e.g. when both sides use arms, but when the opposition to the government does not control any portion of the territory. Disagreement exists on this question: some experts argue that common Article 3 must now be read in conjunction with Protocol II, and that the scope of application of common Article 3 must be the same as that of Protocol II. The better legally founded view, however, is that common Article 3 has maintained its own scope of application and that it has a wider application than that of

Protocol II.

Common Article 3 includes elements which are derived in part from the principles of the rules of warfare and partly from the principles of the protection of the victims of armed conflict. This follows from a reading of the main body of the Article:

1 Persons taking no active part in the hostilities, including members of armed forces who have laid down their arms and those placed hors de combat by sickness, wounds, detention, or any other cause, shall in all circumstances be treated humanely, without any adverse distinction founded on race, colour, religion or faith, sex, birth or wealth, or any other similar criteria.

To this end, the following acts are and shall remain prohibited at any time and any place whatsoever with respect to the above-mentioned persons:

(a) violence to life and person, in particular murder of all kinds, mutilation, cruel treatment and torture;

(b) taking of hostages;

(c) outrages upon personal dignity, in particular humiliating and degrading treatment;

(d) the passing of sentences and the carrying out of executions without previous judgement pronounced by a regularly constituted court, affording all the judicial guarantees which are recognized as indispensable by civilized peoples.

2 The wounded and sick shall be collected and cared for.

This provision is based partly on the 'ratione personae' restriction, according to which belligerents shall leave non-combatants outside the area of operations and refrain from deliberately attacking them; it is also based on the principle that States must ensure the protection of persons in their power. This dimension of the problem is closely related to human rights concerns. The protection of the integrity of the person, the right to life, freedom from torture and maltreatment, as well as freedom from slavery and other denials of freedom, the right to a fair trial and application of the rule of law, are concerns common to humanitarian law and the law of human rights.

2. The international law of human rights

The components of the contemporary normative system of human rights have been outlined above. Whilst formulated as rights, they also entail corresponding obligations for States, which can be divided into the following three categories: the obligations to respect, to protect and to implement human rights. The obligation to respect human rights requires that the State, and all organs of the State, shall abstain from violating the integrity of the individual or his freedom of action. The obligation to protect consists in the State preventing other individuals or groups from violating the integrity, freedom of action, or other human rights of the individual. The obligation to implement consists in the adoption of measures by the State to fulfil, for everyone within its jurisdiction, the needs which are expressed in the human rights law, such as the right to work, to an adequate standard of living, education, health, etc.

The State has therefore a complex role to perform: it must not itself violate the rights of the individuals, but it must be active in order to protect individuals and fulfil their rights. Carrying out their obligations, the governments often will be drawn into conflicts between competing interests and opposing groups. The delicate balance between the respect for the integrity and freedom of individuals, on the one hand, and the obligation to fulfil the tasks incumbent on the State, on the other, is the core of the human rights concern.

With regard to the problems which arise during periods of internal disturbances and tensions, it is important to note that the Human Rights Commission is considering a draft Convention against Torture and other Cruel, Inhuman and Degrading Treatment or Punishment. A Declaration on this matter has already been adopted by the General Assembly.[3] Mention should also be made of the 'Standard Minimum Rules for the Treatment of Prisoners', adopted in 1955 by the First United Nations Congress on the Prevention of Crime and the Treatment of Offenders, and subsequently approved by the Economic and Social Council.[4] Furthermore, the Code of Conduct of Law Enforcement Officials, adopted by the General Assembly in 1979[5] states in its Article 2: 'In the performance of their duty, law enforcement officials shall respect and protect human dignity and maintain and uphold the human rights of all persons.'

One should also mention that in 1984 the Working Group on Detention of the Sub-Commission on the Prevention of Discrimination and Protection of Minorities will discuss the following proposals:

a) *In regard to the period of imprisonment*:
* any arrest followed by custody should be made public without delay or at least be entered in a register;
* the time during which a person is held incommunicado should not exceed a short period prescribed by the emergency law itself;
* in order to protect life and personal freedom, it should not be possible to suspend the procedure of habeas corpus or similar remedies in any situation, including a state of siege or emergency.

b) *In regard to the inalienable right to a fair trial, the following should be guaranteed* :
* a minimum of communication with the defence counsel who should be freely chosen;
* the proceedings should be made public, even if attendance is restricted to the family and, most important, to legal observers who are qualified or appointed by non-governmental organizations.

c) *In regard to sentences*:
* capital punishment should be abolished, particularly where political matters are concerned.

d) *In regard to procedure*:
* any provision of penal law permitting retroactive changes in jurisdiction or procedure shall be suspended when a state of emergency enters into force.

3. The problem of derogation

Article 4 of the Covenant on Civil and Political Rights allows for derogation of some human rights, to a limited extent, 'in time of public emergency which threatens the life of the nation'. This provision may endanger the protection of human rights in cases of internal disturbances and tensions, since it might be alleged that such situations threaten the life of the nation.

However, this is neither the intention nor the way in which this provision is understood by the United Nations. Much attention has been given to this problem, and a major study has been completed recently by a member of the Sub-Commission on the Prevention of Discrimination and Protection of Minorities.[6] In this study, it is pointed out that there are several limitations to the right of derogation. These include:

a) the principle that there must be an exceptional threat ('time of public emergency threatening the life of the nation'). Most tensions do not disturb the life of the nation; they are only the symptom of change through which any nation must go in its evolution. Old social orders fall and new ones emerge, gradually or suddenly, under the impact of industrialization or other reasons. Periods of integration are followed by periods of greater decentralization. A clear distinction must be made between a threat to the life of a nation, on the one hand, and normal changes in the evolution of the nation, on the other;

b) the principle that a state of emergency must be proclaimed. This raises the question of who is entitled to make the proclamation. If the constitutional authorities are replaced by an unpopular military coup, it would be paradoxical if the military government proclaims an emergency—which it has itself created—and derogates from several of the human rights safeguards;

c) the principle of proportionality. Derogations must be no more extensive than what is strictly required by the specific situation. The fact that there have been terrorist acts by non-governmental organs does not allow the government agents to carry out acts which in scope and arbitrariness go far beyond those carried out by terrorists. The problem of proportionality concerns as well the legitimate contents of derogation, as compared to the nature of the threat. The danger of escalation must also be taken into account. Violations of human rights by government agents may lead to counter-violations by members of the public and thus in themselves intensify the 'threat to the nation';

d) the principle of non-discrimination. Derogations must not, directly or indirectly, be effected in a discriminatory way so that particular ethnic, racial, religious, linguistic or social groups are hurt. 'Emergency' as a pretext for suppressing legitimate social and political movements would normally be unacceptable, even though there may be moments when the nature of social or political confrontation has become so acute that a temporary 'cooling-down' may be required;

e) the principle of the non-derogatory nature of certain human rights provisions. The right to life, the prohibition of torture and maltreatment, the prohibition of slavery, the principle of non-retroactivity, the right of everyone to be recognized as a person before the law, and the right to freedom of thought, conscience and religion are inviolable at all times. It is interesting, however, that there is no express prohibition of derogation from due process of law, except when cap punishment is involved. In this regard, Protocol II goes further than the International Covenant on Civil and Political Rights. Human rights instruments need to be improved on this point;

f) the principle that any derogation is transitory and that its sole purpose is to facilitate at the earliest moment the return to full respect for all human rights.

The International Commission of Jurists has recently presented a comprehensive study on this topic entitled: 'States of Emergency: Their Impact on Human Rights'. This study of State practices, as well as the conclusions and observations, deserves close attention.

III The obligation of States to implement the applicable law

The Geneva Conventions contain detailed rules concerning the obligation of States to implement humanitarian law. These include the duty to disseminate the texts of these rules to military and civilian institutions. States also have the obligation to transmit to each other, through the Depositary, the official translations of the Conventions, as well as the laws and regulations they adopt to ensure their application. In particular, they have the obligation to enact penal legislation to provide for effective sanctions against persons who have committed, or ordered to be committed, any grave breaches of the Conventions and the Protocol. As far as Article 3 is concerned, however, 'grave breaches' are not identified.

The obligations of States under the law of human rights are less clear in this regard. Thus, Article 2 of the Covenant on Civil and Political Rights contains an undertaking by States to respect and to ensure to all individuals within their territory and subject to their jurisdiction, the rights recognized in the Convention. They have the obligation to take necessary legislative or other measures to give effect to these rights. Hence, specific obligations depend to a large extent on the discretion of States.

1. Supervising implementation

The ICRC seeks to be kept informed about legislative and other measures taken by States, as well as their programmes for dissemination and education. Common Article 3 does not, however, lend itself to detailed supervision because of its vagueness. Protocol II provides in Article 19 for the widest possible dissemination of its text. The ICRC might attempt to monitor the dissemination of the text of Article 3 in connection with its monitoring of Protocol II, although it has no formal base to do so.

In the international law of human rights, the mechanisms of supervision are evolving slowly. The basic problem here, as it is in humanitarian law in regard to non-international conflicts, is the tension between national sovereignty and international concerns. The attitudes to this problem are not static. A slow and painful progress has taken place by which international procedures have emerged. Three different categories of mechanisms now exist under human rights law:

a) reporting systems, by which the international organs base their supervision on discussion of reports submitted by governments, concerning their human rights performance. In the field of civil and political rights, the Human Rights Committee is the main body;
b) the handling of communications and other allegations regarding violations of human rights, where the Commission and Sub-Commission are the main bodies concerned;
c) the system of individual complaints (by the individual whose rights have been violated). This system is provided for in the Optional Protocol to the Covenant on Civil and Political Rights, which has been ratified by a small number of States.

2. Reporting systems: strengths and weaknesses

All States parties to the Covenant on Civil and Political Rights, the Convention on the Elimination of Racial Discrimination, and the Convention on the Elimination of All Forms of Discrimination against Women, have undertaken to submit reports on the measures they have taken to implement the obligations contained in these instruments. Under Article 40 of the Covenant, they have the obligation to 'describe measures which they have adopted to give effect to the rights recognized in the Covenant' and 'on the progress made in the enjoyment of those rights'. These reports shall 'indicate the factors and difficulties, if any, affecting the implementation' of the Covenant. These reports cannot be limited to constitutions, statutory and other laws, or regulations, but must also refer to facts and practice. No doubt there is much more work to be done in this area. The question of inadequate information, combined with that of the use of additional information, is a major problem. Nevertheless, the reporting system is important and should be given greater attention. Non-governmental organizations should draw the attention of the public to the reports, so that interested groups might react to the information given and inform the experts on the Committee if they hold the information to be inadequate.

3. Reaction to violations

The reporting system consists of a dialogue and it is primarily based on information provided by governments. Some of them may be willing to report on their own shortcomings; few, if any, are willing to report on their own violations of human rights. Since the adoption of the Universal Declaration on Human Rights, a steady and growing stream of communications about violations of human rights has been forwarded to the United Nations. For a very long period, these communications were received but neglected. The breakthrough came in the context of decolonization and the struggle against apartheid. In 1965 the Special Committee on the Situation with Regard to the Implementation of the Declaration on the Granting of Independence to Colonial Countries and Peoples drew the attention of the Commission on Human Rights to evidence submitted by petitioners concerning violations in non-self-governing territories. There was wide support in the United Nations to make the human rights organs respond to these allegations of violations. This was done, first, with regard to South Africa, then with regard to non-self-governing territories, and it was subsequently extended to situations anywhere in the world which appeared to reveal a consistent pattern of gross violations of human rights. The origin of these latter efforts is to be found in Resolutions 8 (XXIII) and 9 (XXIII) of 16 March 1967 of the Commission on Human Rights. These resulted in ECOSOC Resolution 1235 (XVII) of 6 June

1967, in which the Council

* confirmed the Commission's mandate to deal with violations wherever they occur;
* welcomed the Commission's decision to hold an annual debate on violations;
* authorized the Commission and the Sub-Commission to examine information on gross violations contained in communications; and most notably
* decided that the Commission may, after careful examination of the information thus available to it, make a thorough study of situations which reveal a consistent pattern of violations of human rights;
* decided that the Commission may report to the Council on the outcome.

This resolution has gradually given rise to two different procedures, the 'public' and the 'confidential'. The 'public' procedure is based on Human Rights Commission Resolution 8 (XXIII) and the above mentioned ECOSOC resolution; the 'confidential' procedure is based on ECOSOC Resolution 1503 (XLVII).

Under the public procedure, the Sub-Commission may report to the Commission on the occurrence of gross violations of human rights anywhere in the world, on the basis of information provided to it by non-governmental organizations, specialized agencies, governments, or by its own experts and on the basis of replies and comments by the government of the country concerned. The Commission on Human Rights may also base itself on the information obtained, apart from that submitted by the Sub-Commission. The Commission may submit to the Economic and Social Council advice, proposals, reports, and recommendations. Action by the Commission is almost always endorsed by the Council.

In 1970, ECOSOC adopted Resolution 1503 (XLVII) which formalizes a confidential procedure to handle communications. It is not a procedure for individual complaints since it provides no direct standing for the individual or group whose rights have been violated, nor does it provide any redress. The essence of the procedure is to make it possible for the United Nations to initiate a dialogue with governments alleged to engage in gross and consistent violations of human rights. If this dialogue is not possible because of non-cooperation by the governments concerned, or if they continue to engage in gross violations in spite of the dialogue, the Commission can 'go public' by terminating its confidential considerations and reporting publicly on its findings. This has happened in a couple of cases up to now, and the number may be expected to increase in the years to come.

The United Nations has also experimented with other forms of responses to violations. One of these is the Working Group on Enforced or Involuntary Disappearances, established in 1980, to seek and receive information from governments, intergovernmental organizations, humanitarian organizations and other reliable sources. This Working Group has developed a system for tracing the fate of disappeared individuals whose disappearance may be due to the use of force by government authorities or by persons operating with the acquiescence of governments. It has developed a flexible, pragmatic approach which might set a precedent in the United Nations for other activities of a similar nature. This experiment has been strongly influenced and inspired by the work of non-governmental organizations.

The ultimate goal should be the development of an international system for the hearing of complaints by individuals. Such a system is already in existence in the European system, and for those States which have ratified the inter-American Convention. The Optional Protocol to the United Nations Covenant on Civil and Political Rights also provides for individual complaints, but it has been ratified by only a small number of States so far.

4. Sanctions

At present, the possible sanctions against violations of human rights will have to be found in the applicable body of international law—i.e. humanitarian law, or the law of human rights. If by sanction is meant the organized or collective use of force, these are no more available here than in most other fields of international law. The principle of reciprocity, which is a strong underlying factor in the respect for humanitarian law in international armed conflict, does not operate effectively with regard to domestic situations.

In order to have a better understanding of this problem, it is necessary to distinguish between possible international sanctions on the one hand, and domestic sanctions on the other. We are here primarily concerned with international sanctions. Traditionally, international law has been upheld by reciprocal self-interest and to some extent by self-help. In modern international law, the scope for self-help has been significantly limited. In the field of humanitarian law and the law of human rights, the self-interest of other States is too weak a factor. Nor have centralized executive organs in the international community been developed which can implement measures of deprivation directed against States violating the law, or measures of assistance to the victims.

There is, however, a continuous and expanding debate about the possibility of organizing sanctions. One setting of this debate is international development collaboration. Individual States as well as groups of States debate the possibility of establishing rules for the denial of development assistance in cases of severe human rights violations. Some countries, such as the United States, have incorporated such provisions in their national legislation; others, such as the members of the European Communities, are in the process of discussing the possibility of formulating guidelines for the denial of assistance in cases of grave violations. It must be concluded, however, that these efforts have reached a very low level of sophistication and consistency, and that we are far from a situation in which generally accepted criteria for sanctions can be adopted.

The only available international sanction is that of publicity. The impact of publicity depends, however, on two factors: the degree to which condemnation is shared by the members of the international community, in particular by the most important States; and to what extent this publicity is based on clear and unequivocal findings, or whether it consists only in competing claims and allegations.

These two factors are inter-related. The better the procedures of supervision, investigation and fact-finding can be developed, the more likely it is that the publicity arising out of such activities will have an impact. It is well known that human rights policy is motivated often by the search for political benefits rather than by humanitarian concerns. In order to eliminate the misuse of allegations of human rights violations, it is important that bodies enjoying high international respect and recognition be able to determine the merits of the claims.

The ICRC pursues a policy of non-publicity in most instances. This has been found useful in order to maintain a dialogue with the governments concerned. On the other hand, it precludes the use of information obtained by the ICRC as an instrument in responding to violations. Other non-governmental organizations, like Amnesty International, pursue the opposite policy: maximum publicity about alleged violations which Amnesty considers to be sufficiently well substantiated. This publicity has been of great significance, but it also has its weaknesses.

As pointed out above, the United Nations and the regional inter-governmental organizations have developed certain mechanisms for the supervision of the implementation of human rights, and for the response to human rights violations.

The reporting system does not necessarily bring out all the facts, particularly those which testify to serious violations of human rights by the government concerned. The United Nations has therefore found it increasingly necessary to resort to its own fact-finding. Collecting evidence helps first of all to clarify disputed facts presented in the context of allegations concerning human rights violations. Such allegations can be made for good or for bad motives. It is essential that the international community should be able to assess allegations properly, and in this way to avoid improper condemnation of governments and to strengthen the impact of international condemnation when serious violations can reasonably be proved to have taken place.

Several devices have been developed for the purpose of fact-finding. Special Rapporteurs have been appointed; working groups have been established, semi-judicial bodies have been brought into operation. All of these require a legal base for their various activities.

Since 1967, substantial evolution has taken place, including the development of a number of devices to clarify at least to some extent the veracity of allegations of human rights violations. Nevertheless, the system is heavily dependent upon the cooperation of the government concerned. On-site observation is impossible without the consent of the government concerned; failure to respond or false information by the government can also frustrate the efforts of the international human rights bodies to determine the truth.

However, the picture is not only negative. Governments often see a usefulness in submitting to international investigations. It can help to quell exaggerated claims of violations, and it can also help to make the international community aware of the problems facing that particular government.

IV Conclusions

There is a fundamental gap in existing international law: the lack of provisions which address themselves to particular situations arising during internal conflicts that are not armed conflicts. For non-international armed conflicts, Protocol II provides a modicum of rules of protection; for armed conflicts falling below the threshold of Protocol II there is still Article 3 common to the Geneva Conventions. When, however, the opposition groups or any person or group of persons in conflict with the authorities do not resort to the use of arms, no provisions are available.

Admittedly, the law of human rights is applicable in all of these situations, but these provisions do not address themselves to the establishment of limitations and constraints in confrontations between the authorities and opposing groups within the State. As soon as the opposition falls into the power of government agents, the human rights provisions become applicable. Thus, they are entitled to respect for their life and integrity, a fair trial and the application of the rule of law.

But during confrontation prior to such apprehension there are few direct rules, and the most that can be done in these situations is to apply the spirit behind the human rights provisions. The right to life should apply also when police forces are confronted with unarmed demonstrators or strikers. They cannot be entitled to shoot except in cases of genuine self-defence. But regulations for this problem are almost non-existent in international law. There is even more of a gap in contemporary human rights law with regard to the obligations of individuals and groups opposed to the government in the event of any period of confrontation. The very general reference in Article 29 of the Universal Declaration provides little in terms of restraint.

For these reasons, international supervision and international responses to violations as well as the imposition of sanctions are little developed. Efforts to improve this situation are being made by both the ICRC and the United Nations. With regard to the former, the concern with prisoners has been expanded to deal also with situations of disturbances and tensions; as for the United Nations the concern with extra-legal executions and disappeared persons is relevant in this regard.

There can be no doubt, however, that these efforts are insufficient. Nor is there any doubt that serious human suffering takes place during internal conflicts, whether armed or non-armed. Massacres, large-scale disappearances, and confinement of political dissidents to psychiatric institutions occur frequently even in the absence of open, armed conflict.

V Epilogue: The need for a new institution to develop and promote humanitarian norms in situations of internal disturbances and tensions

In his report to the Independent Commission on Humanitarian Issues, Antonio Cassese—dealing with the problem of non-international armed conflicts—has suggested the establishment of a 'Comité de Sages' with humanitarian and supervisory functions. Such a body might also be called upon to fill some of the gaps which have been shown to exist in the context of internal disturbances and tensions.

The task of this Committee would be twofold: first, it should take the initiative in the adoption of new rules in this field. These would have to be adopted either in the form of binding instruments (conventions and protocols) or by declarations. In either case, they could be adopted only by the General Assembly or by a diplomatic conference. But the initiative might well be taken by a voluntary body.

The new body of law would have to find its inspirations in part in the humanitarian law developed for situations of armed conflict, and in part in human rights law. It would have to deal, in particular, with those regulations which should apply in the context of confrontations and interactions typical of situations of disturbances and tension.

The second task would be to promote the implementation of these new rules, and to assist in their application. Such assistance could take the form of providing impartial fact-finding services, consultations to all sides, to the extent consent is forthcoming, in particular from governments; and to provide good offices, including mediation, with regard to the humanitarian concerns involved in these confrontations.

The operation of such a body, acting voluntarily, and only on the basis of consent, might considerably help in preventing the escalation of such disturbances into national and even international conflagrations, and it might considerably lessen the suffering which occurs during a period of tension. What is more, it might help those involved to find a humane and rational solution to their differences without resorting to violence and extensive repression.

Notes

1. Conference of Government Experts, vol. V, Protection of Victims of Non-International Armed Conflicts, ICRC 1971, p. 79.
2. See Jan Egeland, 'Humanitarian Initiative Against Political Disappearances', Henry Dunant Institute 1982, p. 30.
3. General Assembly Resolution 3452 (XXX).
4. ECOSOC Res. 663 C (XXIV) and 2076 (LXIII).
5. General Assembly Resolution 34/169.
6. Mrs. N. Questiaux, 'Study of the implications for human rights of recent developments covering situations known as states of siege or emergency'—doc. E/CN.4/SUB.2/1982/15.

Enquiry Mechanisms and Violations of Humanitarian Law

Some suggestions on how to improve their effectiveness

Konstantin Obradovic

Contents

Konstantin Obradovic is the Director of Research at the Institute of International Politics and Economics, Belgrade. He was a member of the Yugoslav Delegation at the Diplomatic Conference on the Reaffirmation and Development of International Humanitarian Law. He is the author of numerous works in Serbo-Croatian on humanitarian law, and of 'The Protection of Civilian Populations in International Armed Conflicts' (in 'The New Humanitarian Law of Armed Conflict', 1979).

IV—Suggestions for Improving the System
    1. Political action
        a) revalorization of humanitarian law
        b) depoliticizing the violations problem
    2. Legal action
        a) exchange of information between the contracting parties
        b) legal basis for collective action
        c) optional clauses, obligatory clauses
        d) creation of a new institution

I Introductory Remarks

It seems necessary at the outset to stress two important factors which may limit the scope of the suggestions we wish to make, but which serve as a framework for the ideas on which our suggestions are based.

1. Humanitarian protection and the absence of political will for its application

Firstly, it should be pointed out that the level of protection afforded to victims of armed conflict depends on the type of armed conflict in question: whereas the level of protection may be termed as satisfactory in international conflicts, it is far less so in the case of internal conflicts, and is non-existent in situations of internal disturbances and tensions because such situations do not correspond to the definition of 'armed conflict not of an international character', even though weapons may be (and often are) used. Although it has been necessary to apply different legal regimes to the various types of armed conflict in the past, such differentiation no longer seems logical today. It may even be said that such differences in approach are contradictory to the spirit and concept of human rights as generally accepted today. Indeed, one of the objectives of the efforts aimed at establishing a 'new international humanitarian order' is a uniform regime of protection for the individual whenever armed force is used. Clearly, we are still a long way from this objective, especially when one considers the most recent revision of humanitarian law by the Diplomatic Conference of 1974-1977, when it was decided that the different regimes should be retained. With regard to the issues of interest to this paper, the practical consequences thereof are that the mechanisms of international control only exist in the most highly developed field of humanitarian law, that governing international conflicts. We should, therefore, concentrate primarily—if not exclusively—on the effectiveness of these existing mechanisms if we are to advance our ideas for their practical implementation.

It should also be pointed out that the ineffectiveness of the existing institutions is due much less to flaws in the law itself than to the lack of political will on the part of States to make use of such institutions. This lack of will is the key to the problem, and the means must be found to prompt States into implementing these institutions. Such means do exist and are of both a political and a legal nature. Quite simply, States should be placed in a position where it is difficult for them to deny certain fundamental obligations emanating from general international law as being fundamental provisions of humanitarian law; they should be denied the right to remain passive in situations where allegations of serious violations of humanitarian law are made, even in cases where such allegations have not been proven by adequate procedures.

In other words, one of the first steps would be to prevent the international community as a whole from remaining indifferent to violations of humanitarian law and to remind its members—practically all of whom are bound by the Geneva Conventions—that their obligations do not merely consist of their individual respect for humanitarian law, but that all States party to the Conventions and Protocols must take action so that the humanitarian regulations are respected in general.

2. Implementation of Institutions and Revision of Existing Laws

The first step towards the implementation of currently 'non-operational' institutions, therefore, consists of making members of the international community aware of their obligation to take action when confronted with violations of humanitarian law. They should also be made aware of the fact that these obligations are already contained in laws enabling concrete action. Action of this kind should lead to the implementation of the heretofore neglected provisions of humanitarian law, thereby paving the way—albeit indirectly—for the direct application of provisions concerning 'control' and the 'identification of violations'.

As a second step, measures could be envisaged for the revision of existing law and the subsequent reshaping of implementation mechanisms. In any event, a proliferation of regulations and institutions serves no purpose unless it is accompanied by effective means for their implementation. This fact, frequently confirmed in international practice, has led us to present our suggestions with caution, both with regard to what appears to be possible and feasible today, and what is desirable in the future—provided a favourable political and legal environment is established beforehand.

The use of armed force is a part of our times despite the longstanding formal and absolute prohibition thereof imposed by international law. Although the international community has managed to avoid a conflict of a global and generalized nature, it has not succeeded in preventing the outbreak of several hundred conflicts of an essentially internal nature since the end of World War II. Although limited geographically, none of these wars have lost any of the 'total war' aspects inherent in the last world conflict.

II The Development of Humanitarian Law

Humanitarian law, perhaps one of the most carefully formulated branches of international law, is almost entirely codified. Its codification was initiated in the mid-1800s, and currently represents a veritable 'code of conduct' comprising some 600 meticulously worded articles. Consequently, it is difficult to claim ignorance of its content, and thereby to make excuses for poor application, and even less so for breaches.

1. Humanization of the Laws of Armed Conflict and Military Necessity

Nearly 40 years ago, the fundamental principles of humanitarian law were defined by the Nurenberg Tribunal as norms of 'jus cogens' and thereby binding for all States, including States not parties to conventional obligations. Serious breaches thereof, termed as 'war crimes' or crimes 'against humanity', became a source of individual penal responsibility—an exceptional phenomenon in international law.

The most recent adaptations of humanitarian law, particularly those of 1949 and 1974-1977, were shaped in accordance with the demands of an international society profoundly changed by the Charter. These adaptations put those regulations on a par with the achievements obtained in the protection of the individual. The former 'laws of war'—the new denomination 'humanitarian law' being far from fortuitous—were thus associated with human rights. Humanitarian law is even considered by some to be a part of human rights, to the extent that its fundamental concept has been transformed. This transformation is reflected both in the approach to and in the spirit of contemporary humanitarian law, where military necessity is subordinated to humanitarian requirements.

2. Common Interest of the International Community

The 'humanization' of the laws of armed conflict, combined with the suppression of military necessity, is merely a reflection and consequence of general developments in international law. What distinguishes this law from traditional international law is the increasingly stressed protection of what may be termed the 'common interest' of international society. Certain regulations are placed at the summit of the hierarchy of the norms of international law. This is because it is in the interest of the international community as a whole that these regulations be respected owing to their subject matter: these are the norms which guarantee the maintainance of peace and international security, those prohibiting acts of aggression, and those concerning the fundamental rights of the individual.

This position is supported by both the doctrine and the International Court of Justice. In 'Barcelona Traction, Light and Power Company Limited' (second phase) the Court declared that:

> . . .a distinction must be made between the obligations of States to the international community as a whole, and the obligations towards another Stat. . .By their very nature, the former concern all States. Bearing in mind the importance of the laws in question, all States may be considered to have a legal interest in the protectionv of these laws.

Specifying that the obligations in question are 'erga omnes' and quoting, as an example, the fundamental rights of the individual, the Court concludes that:

> . . .some of the corresponding laws of protection have been integrated
> into general international law; others are conferred by international
> instruments of a universal, or quasi-universal character.[1]

The International Law Commission was in favour of this new
trend in international law. In its draft articles on the 'Responsibility
of States for internationally illicit actions' it took a step further
by recommending that a distinction be made between 'offences'
and 'international crimes', the latter being imputable not only to
individuals but to the State per se. In its commentary on draft Article
19, and basing it on the above-mentioned ICJ judgement and other
elements emanating from practice and international law doctrine,
the Commission reaches some extremely important conclusions.
In the view of the International Law Commission, a limited number
of international obligations do exist which, by their very object,
are important to the international community as a whole; all States
have a vested interest in respecting these obligations. Therefore,
responsibility for violation of these obligations is not merely a commitment towards the State which is a direct victim of the violation. It is also a commitment towards all the other members of the
international community because any State victim of such violation is justified in pointing out the responsibility of the offending
State. This would amount to a sort of 'actio popularis' by the international community against them.

If international practice is considered in this light, it may be said
that activities of this kind already take place: the measures recommended by the General Assembly against South Africa's practice
of apartheid is one example. The mechanism recommended by the
General Assembly has not been prescribed by legal channels, but
there is no doubt that the legal foundations of the action itself are
based on the fact that the practice of apartheid represents a violation of a law which affects the 'common interest' of international
society and entitles its members to take action.

Although there is a difference between the right to do something,
the ability to react, and the obligation to act, in issues concerning
humanitarian law it appears to us that such distinctions are irrele-
vant and that 'rights' and 'obligations' are one and the same.

3. Humanitarian Law and Human Rights
Considering the current importance of the protection of human

rights within the hierarchy of international law regulations in general, and the obligations of States towards the implementation of and respect for these regulations, a human rights approach is fundamental in all questions relating to humanitarian law.

If humanitarian law is to be considered a part of human rights (which is theoretically justifiable despite certain opposition from the doctrinal point of view), and if the examination of all problems linked to its implementation is considered in this light, then the obligations of States not to remain indifferent when confronted with serious allegations of breaches of humanitarian law become more evident. Equally well, such obligations are also contained in humanitarian law itself, particularly in the Geneva Conventions of 1949.

4. Humanitarian Law Norms as Norms of 'Jus Cogens'

Both the Geneva Conventions and the Hague Conventions are universally recognized legal instruments. Their legal value is undeniable, to the extent that they may be considered to be rules admitted by all civilized States and regarded by them as the codified expression of the laws and customs of war—just as the Hague Regulations were recognized by the Nuremberg Tribunal in the past. The essential provisions contained in the Geneva Conventions are certainly norms of 'jus cogens'. And there is no doubt that the regulations governing grave breaches, and therefore international crimes, fall within this category. The Contracting Parties took a solemn pledge in Article 1 common to all four Geneva Conventions, not only to apply and respect these regulations and to respect them within their individual competence, but also to ensure their respect.

Such an obligation must be seen today in the context of general obligations concerning the respect of human rights. The obligation to 'ensure respect' for the Conventions in all circumstances is thus the obligation of every Contracting Party to take action, either individually or jointly with the others, so that respect for humanitarian law may be assured.

III The Implementation of Humanitarian Law

The basic concept forming the foundations of all philosophy

concerning the implementation of humanitarian law is completed by a control system which is atypical of all other branches of international law. Indeed, other legal instruments do not provide special means of control for their implementation: the contracting parties are expected to fulfil their obligations themselves and it is the responsibility of the State victim of a violation to assert its own rights. In humanitarian law, however, provision is made for special means of control because the application of and the respect for these regulations is in the interest of the international community, especially regulations directly applicable to armed conflicts. This system should thus be put into effect from the onset of any conflict.

1. Preventive Control

This form of control is essentially one of prevention and its principal role is to prevent violations. Indeed, the primary goal of humanitarian law is to protect individuals from the dangers of hostilities, although this objective cannot be obtained unless the spirit and letter of the law is applied.

a) The role of the Protecting Power and its substitute—Control is effected through the offices of the Protecting Power, a State appointed by one of the Parties to the conflict, with the consent of the adverse party. The role of the Protecting Power is to safeguard the interests of the Party which appointed it, and to lend its support to the application of humanitarian law by the adverse party to which it is accredited and, at the same time, to undertake the control of such application. In other words, the Protecting Power is responsible for the protection of nationals of the State whose interests it safeguards against any violation by the adverse party. At the same time, it collaborates with the adverse party in order to prevent any such violation. In the absence of a Protecting Power (which is always a possibility owing to the need for consent by the adverse party), this role is conferred upon a 'substitute' for the Protecting Power. Here again, however, the substitute cannot operate without the consent of the conflicting powers.

b) The humanitarian role of the ICRC—In addition to the Protecting Powers system, but parallel to it, humanitarian activities are undertaken by the ICRC (or by another impartial humanitarian organization). The purpose of these activities is to protect the victims of the armed conflict. Referred to in a provision common to the Conventions (articles 9/9/9/10), the purpose of these activities is not to control the application of the Conventions, but only to assist persons protected by the Conventions without discrimination as to their association with either of the Parties to the conflict.

In practice, however, the results obtained by ICRC activities strongly resemble those of effective control. Indeed, experience has shown that the mere presence of neutral delegates, such as those from the ICRC, on the scene of military operations will frequently act as a deterrent and prevent the belligerents from committing breaches and violations of humanitarian law. Nonetheless, the consent of the parties to the conflict is essential to the implementation of these humanitarian activities.

In the long run, however, implementation of the preventive control system by the Protecting Power or its substitute, as specified in the articles common to the Conventions (8/8/8/9 and 10/10/10/11) and in Article 5 of Protocol I, remains optional.

2. 'Ex post facto' Control

a) Conciliation procedures —The same applies to 'ex post facto' control, that is, control activities to be undertaken in the case of alleged violations of humanitarian law. The Conventions provide for two eventualities: even before accusations of violating humanitarian law are made, when faced with a dispute between the Parties to the conflict over the application or interpretation of the Conventions, a conciliation procedure should be undertaken through the good offices of the Protecting Powers for the resolution of such a dispute. (In the absence of a Protecting Power or substitute, however, it is obviously difficult to imagine how this procedure would function). Here again, however, once these good offices are offered, they must be accepted by the parties concerned.

b) Enquiry procedures and the International Fact-Finding Commission —The second possibility for the repression of violations is described by the provisions contained in Articles 52/53/132/149. At the request of a Party to the conflict, an enquiry procedure may be initiated if claims are made that violations have been committed. According to the above-mentioned articles, the enquiry should be obligatory, but the interested parties must agree beforehand on the procedure to be followed. Failing this, the parties must agree on the choice of an umpire who will decide upon the procedure to be followed. No provisions have been made, however, for cases where the parties fail to reach an agreement on either the procedure to be followed or the choice of an umpire. One may safely conclude, therefore, that the enquiry will not take place and this is indeed what happens in practice.

In order to avoid the relinquishment of the enquiry through lack of agreement on the procedure to be followed, the authors of Protocol I proposed the establishment of a special body having the competence to carry out such enquiries: the International Fact-Finding Commission. Article 90 of the Protocol revives an idea which already figured on the agenda of the Diplomatic Conference of 1949 and which is described in the Commentary of the First Convention of the ICRC.[3] Only a permanent body, operating on a quasi-automatic basis and independent of the consent of the parties, could be an effective tool for enquiring into and establishing the facts concerning alleged violations. Yet this idea was discarded in 1949, only to be accepted—although only partially—in 1977. The automatic or quasi-automatic element which would serve to remove the obstacle (i.e. the prior consent of the parties concerned) from the implementation of mechanisms of this kind was not accepted.

Thus, Article 90 provides for the creation of a permanent Commission which has the competence to enquire into any facts alleged to be a grave breach of the Conventions or the Protocol. The Commission is to consist of 15 members, elected in their personal capacity by representatives of the High Contracting Parties, having recognized ' "ipso facto" and without special agreement, in relation to any other High Contracting Party accepting the same obligation' the competence of the Commission. Quite clearly, this formula strongly resembles the so-called 'optional' clause of acceptance of the jurisdiction of the International Court of Justice. This means that the High Contracting Parties do not automatically accept the competence of the Commission by acceding to the Protocol; they must do so expressis verbis, and a minimum of '0 such declarations is necessary before the Commission can be established. The declaration of acceptance may be made at any time, either at the time of ratifying or acceding to the Protocol, or at any subsequent time; in other words, even in situations where a dispute already exists. The Commission also has the competence to enquire into any other violation, including those not defined by the Protocol as 'grave'. In situations of this kind, the Commission cannot take action 'ex-officio', but must obtain the consent of all Parties concerned.

Although Article 90 allows the parties to propose the procedure of their choice, sub-paragraphs 3-5 make provision for the recommended procedure. This procedure is described in great detail and is undertaken by a Chamber appointed for each case in point. Consequently, it is virtually identical to the procedure normally applied by a court of justice or other legal authority. Yet the results of the enquiry are not termed as a 'judgement'. Rather, the Commission's 'findings' are submitted to the Parties concerned and are not made public without the consent of the Parties to the conflict. Because the Commission is also competent to . . . facilitate, through its good offices, the restoration of an attitude of respect for the Conventions and this Protocol, the findings of the Commission (if, indeed, it is established that a violation has taken place) should have a consequence; that is, the violation should cease and the law should be correctly applied thereafter. However, because the Commission is a fact-finding body, it may only establish the responsibility of the offending party indirectly; it may not establish the consequences of such responsibility, nor the conditions applicable to such responsibility. It is the responsibility of the State victim of a violation to apply for justice before another competent legal authority (international arbitration, ICJ).

Two other important factors should also be stressed: Firstly, Article 90 does not question the validity of the provisions concerning enquiries contained in the Conventions. The parties may choose between applying these provisions and thereby settling the affair between themselves, or addressing the Commission. Secondly, it seems logical that even those States which have not acceded to the Protocol but which are party to the Geneva Conventions, may request the Commission to enquire into an affair by accepting its competence through declarations specific to the concrete case.

Quite obviously, the Commission itself must first be created. To date, however, only six States have made the declaration according to Article 90—a far cry from the 20 States necessary for the establishment of the International Fact-Finding Commission.

This overview of the various provisions contained in humanitarian law concerning the control of its applications and enquiries into possible violations thereof leads us to draw several conclusions. Firstly, what we have termed as preventive control and 'ex post facto' control, are merely two parts of the same system, established in humanitarian law for the purpose of ensuring its full application for the benefit of protected persons. Both parts of this system should, therefore, be considered as a whole and appropriate steps should be taken to ensure they function entirely as a whole. The second conclusion is that the law, per se, is comprehensive. In other words, it should not be considered as incomplete, thereby lending itself to abuses, or criticized for not presenting satisfactory guarantees to those who, acting out of good faith, are willing to apply the relevant provisions contained therein. Lastly, we conclude that this system lacks one essential element: it is not obligatory. This applies both to the norms concerning the activities of the Protecting Power and its substitute, and to the mechanisms for enquiry: all things considered, they are, and remain, optional. Even the most peaceful States are extremely reluctant to 'tie their hands' prematurely by accepting obligations such as those contained in Article 90 of Protocol I. It should be recalled that, during the Diplomatic Conference of 1974-1977, several attempts were made to render the activities of the Protecting Power automatic, and the mechanism contained in Article 90 obligatory. All these attempts failed because of the categorical opposition by one group of States. Although a minority, this group was a powerful one. The 'political clout' of the States in question, combined with the tacit consent of the other participants at the Conference, ultimately resulted in the rejection of these proposals.

IV Suggestions for Improving the System

If the vicious circle created by the States' lack of political will is to be cast aside, one conclusion commands attention: once again, the law must be reshaped, so that the relevant institutions are automatically rendered obligatory. Before an initiative of this kind can be undertaken, however, the international climate (both from the political and the legal points of view) must be in favour of such an enterprise. Indeed, it is essential that the very 'politics' of the international community be changed, both with regard to humanitarian law and its application, and particularly with regard to violations of the law. This backdrop should be borne in mind when considering the initial measures we recommend in order to rectify the current situation.

1. Political Action

a) Revalorization of humanitarian law —A starting poing would be a political action, based on the 'revalorization' of humanitarian law. We should not close our eyes to the fact that mankind (as well as States) has lost faith in a law which they see as being only rarely applied. The objective of such action should be the adoption of the human rights approach for the consideration of all issues relating to humanitarian law and its application. Such action should also aim towards the propagation of the law through ratification of the two Protocols additional to the Geneva Conventions, which constitute the most highly developed expression of humanitarian law and serve specifically to highlight the human rights approach.

b) Depoliticizating the violations problem —The recommended action should also strive for another goal: 'depoliticizing' the violations problem and instead considering it on a strictly legal basis. This would be possible only if States decided to take action, both individually and collectively, in their capacity as contracting parties to the Geneva Conventions and Protocols; in other words, as subjects of humanitarian law.

2. Legal Action

Parallel with this long-term political activity, concrete action in the legal sense of the term is also possible as soon as an armed conflict breaks out. Indeed, the contracting parties to the Geneva Conventions are internationally obliged to take action: to act in order to safeguard the 'common interest' of international society, that is, in order to safeguard the fundamental rights of individuals endangered by the use of weapons; and to act in order to 'ensure respect' for humanitarian law.

a) Exchange of information between the contracting parties — An initial step in this direction would be an exchange of information between the contracting parties concerning the situation on the battlefield vis--vis the application of humanitarian law and the provisions relating to the functioning of the Protecting Power system in particular. It would be wrong to claim that States do not have concrete information concerning alleged violations. An exchange of information of this kind could—and should—take place during meetings in Berne, through diplomatic representatives of the contracting parties accredited thereto. Representatives of the depositary and from the ICRC should also be invited to attend these meetings, especially as the ICRC always keeps abreast of such situations and its advice would serve a useful purpose with regard to the measures to be taken.

The purpose of meetings of this kind, therefore, would not only be an exchange of information; the meetings would also provide a forum for consultations on the information received so that, if need be, decisions may be made on the action to be taken if the control system fails. One may safely assume that not all the contracting parties would participate in these meetings. Initially, it is unimportant whether the meetings are held on an official or unofficial basis. What matters is that a 'collective' of contracting parties is convened—no matter how few attend; that this collective proves willing to fulfil its obligations concerning the promotion of the application of humanitarian law; and that it starts to take action, thereby enabling the establishment of a control mechanism by means of the Protecting Power.

The results of these meetings could be reaffirmed through a series of individual representations, undertaken through diplomatic channels in the capital cities of the parties to the conflict. Alternatively, a joint representation could be presented by the depositary of the Conventions on behalf of all the parties concerned. Another alternative would be a combination of both these methods. The object thereof would amount to the same: to stress the merits of such action based on the obligations provided for in Article 1 common to the Conventions; to call upon the parties to the conflict to fulfil their obligations with regard to the Protecting Power; and lastly, to offer the good offices for the choice of Protecting Powers and their possible substitutes. Steps of this kind could be renewed as and when necessary; but the essential factor lies in the fact that the 'militant nucleus' of the contracting parties insists on—as opposed to desists from—all available means, including the possibility of concerted action within the General Assembly. It is likely that this kind of pressure on the parties to the conflict would produce results.

b) Legal basis for collective action —Similar action should be taken by the contracting parties in cases where accusations of violating humanitarian law are made, although in this case such action should be grounded on a wider legal basis. Realistically speaking, grave breaches amount to war crimes, or crimes against humanity, and are thus punishable both internationally and by the internal laws of most States. Thus, in addition to Article 1 common to the Conventions, the contracting parties could find other elements in general international law which serve as grounds for their action. Not to mention the provisions contained in Article 89 of Protocol I, according to which, in situations of serious violations of humanitarian law '. . . the High Contracting Parties undertake to act, jointly or individually, in cooperation with the United Nations and in conformity with the United Nations Charter'. Collective action by the contracting parties in situations of this kind would, first and foremost, result in the insistence that an enquiry take place, without necessitating a decision on the basic issues.

If all proposals for an enquiry are systematically rejected, is the 'collective' authorized to make an enquiry without the consent of the parties concerned? The answer to this question should be affirmative. International law does not prohibit States from making declarations about a given situation which concerns the application of the law. By cooperating with the consenting party and according to a procedure generally accepted in international law, an enquiry into the facts for the purpose of evaluating the proof submitted can in no way be considered an illicit act—even if one of the parties concerned refuses to comply. For example, the United Nations have made several enquiries into the situation in the Arab territories occupied by Israel and, through its resolutions, the General Assembly has frequently made declarations on humanitarian law violations which have been identified in this way. Furthermore, the contracting parties to the Geneva Conventions have the authority to take action of this kind through their obligation to 'ensure respect' for humanitarian law. The results of the enquiry would obviously be limited to findings and the identification of facts, and would in no way be binding upon the party which refused the enquiry. But the moral and political weight of a conclusion of this kind should not be underestimated—not only vis-à-vis the offending party, but also with respect to all parties to the conflict, both as far as the conflict in question is concerned and with regard to any future conflicts. It goes without saying that it is in the interest of the protected persons themselves that enquiries of this kind should only be undertaken as an extreme measure. They should be used for the purpose of ensuring that parties respect the law, and the appropriateness of such action should always be taken into account.

We have presented our ideas for a general legal basis for 'collective action', both with regard to the establishment of the Protecting Power system and with regard to enquiries. We should add that the idea was also considered by the authors of Protocol I; indeed, Article 7 stipulates:

> The depositary of the Protocol shall convene a meeting of the High Contracting Parties, at the request of one or more of the said Parties and upon the approval of the majority of the said Parties, to consider general problems concerning the application of the Conventions and of the Protocol.

Humanitarian law, therefore, contains a specific obligation which commits the parties to take action in accordance with the procedures we recommend. But because only 59 States have ratified Protocol I to date, the full weight of this provision is not yet generally apparent in humanitarian law. We believe, however, that action of this kind would be acceptable even in the absence of the provision and, moreover, that a meeting convened by the parties to the Protocol in accordance with Article 7 would clearly remain open to all parties to the Geneva Conventions.

Meetings of this kind could also apply in the case of internal conflicts. In such cases, implementation of the Protecting Power system would be impossible, let alone the enquiries procedure. Yet, there is nothing to prevent the contracting parties from convening a meeting in such cases, again in accordance with Article 1 common to the Conventions, but this time in association with Article 3 which binds the contracting parties to respect minimum humanitarian principles even in the case of armed conflict not of an international character. It is essential to demonstrate that the community of subjects of humanitarian law is concerned with all situations where human rights are jeopardized.

Posturing of this kind by the parties to the Geneva Conventions would, in our opinion, have several advantages. Firstly, the contracting parties would fulfil a fundamental obligation of humanitarian law incurred by them upon acceding to the Geneva Conventions. Secondly, it would lead to depoliticizing the problem of the application of humanitarian law and possible violations thereof which, in our view, is an extremely important factor. Lastly, an attitude of this kind would strengthen the credibility of humanitarian law and would create a positive atmosphere for its application and for the implementation of the control system as a whole. One of the results thereof would be to clarify not only the legal elements involved, but also the political, moral and psychological elements, thereby prompting States into willingly supporting the proposed system. It is to be hoped, therefore, that these initial measures would lead to a change in the situation which, in turn, would have a positive effect on the behaviour of the parties to the conflict and their attitude towards the establishment of the control mechanism, including the enquiries procedure. All these measures, however, are clearly palliative.

c) Optional clauses, obligatory clauses —A second phase would consist of measures aimed at reshaping the law and, if possible, changing the institutions thereof by rendering their mechanisms obligatory. This second phase would only be feasible if the political will exists.

In this context, a first suggestion would be to revise the Conventions and Protocol I. A revision of this kind would not affect the existing institutions and mechanisms, but would convert the currently optional clauses into obligatory clauses for all contracting States purely by ratification of or adhesion to the revised legal instruments. An extension of their competence to include the field of application of Protocol II—that is, to non-international conflicts— is not unthinkable, but may be difficult to implement. It would be difficult for any State, no matter how 'humanitarian' it may be, to accept the fact that one or several third powers may assume the role of Protecting Powers for the purpose of controlling the application of humanitarian law; it would be harder still to accept that enquiries into possible violations would be carried out by such powers, thereby placing the legal government and the insurgents on an equal footing.

d) Creation of a new institution —Yet, a further possibility may also be envisaged: that of leaving the positive side of the law as is, and adding a new institution to the current legal edifice—a sort of 'universal substitute for the Protecting Power', which would also assume the role of a fact-finding body in the case of alleged violations.

While part of the laws of armed conflict, a legal instrument of this kind could be prepared by an international conference convened by the United Nations. The initiative could be launched at a meeting between the parties to the Geneva Conventions, but the Conference itself should be held under the aegis of the United Nations. This is because, in our opinion, the new institution should be part of the United Nations family. Proceedings could be based on the recent Convention on so-called 'conventional' weapons, which was concluded in Geneva in 1980.

With respect to the institutional aspect, such a body would be a specialized agency, rather like the United Nations High Commissioner for Refugees. In other words, the agency would be open to all States in their double capacity as members of the United Nations and parties to the Geneva Conventions. Provision could also be made so that even countries which are not members of the United Nations but which are bound by the Conventions (Switzerland, for example) could take part.

Generally speaking, the agency would be competent to deal with all issues concerning the protection of the fundamental rights of individuals in the case of armed conflict. It would commence operations at the onset of an armed conflict; that is, in accordance with the principles and rules which determine the time from which humanitarian law should be applied. Within the framework of its general competence, it would act in accordance with a human rights approach, which means it would monitor respect for human rights in the widest sense of the term. Practically speaking, its actions would consist of making contact with the parties to the conflict in order to ensure maximum protection of human rights. It may be appropriate to make provision for permanent representation of the agency in the principal geographical regions, or even in the capital cities of the member countries, as is the custom with the other specialized agencies.

Because the agency's general competence would in no way contain measures to 'force the hand' of the States in question, it may even be possible to extend its competence to include non-international conflicts. Without acting as a veritable 'control' organization, its general competence would be none other than an international 'presence' in armed conflicts. This presence alone, as we have seen in the case of the ICRC activities, serves to ensure that the parties to the conflict refrain from straying too far from the path prescribed by the law.

The agency would also be bestowed with special competences: preventive control and 'ex post facto' control, both of which should function as a whole. These special competences would, therefore, also include the right to perform the activities of the Protecting Power's 'universal substitute', as well as those of the fact-finding body. Any development of the specialized agency idea would leave the present Conventions and Protocol I system intact, thereby enabling States to make use of this system as they deem fit. If the system provided for by humanitarian law fails to function, after a given time limit (30 days after the onset of the conflict, for example) the agency would commence operations and would immediately assume responsibility for the functions normally attributed to the Protecting Power.

The agency should also be in a position to take action in cases where a dispute cannot be resolved by the methods and means prescribed by current humanitarian law. Here again, once a reasonable time has elapsed since the allegation of a serious breach, and in the event that no verification of the accusation has been made, the agency's enquiry mechanism would start operations.

A specialized agency of this kind could be based on the model presented in Article 90 of Protocol I. The impartiality of such an agency is essential, and sufficient guarantees must be made so that the rights of the parties concerned are fully respected. The results of the enquiries would merely consist of a presentation of the facts, similar to the findings provided for in Article 90 of Protocol I. It seems reasonable, none the less, that provision be made for a follow-up to these findings; that is, the 'determination' of the responsibility which would, in all likelihood, emanate from the presentation of facts. As the 'common interest' would be at issue, the ICJ would doubtless have the competence to examine the question without obligatory competence and parties would have the option to address themselves to the Court if need be.

The special competences of the agency would be 'automatic'.

In other words, the agency would act 'ex officio' as soon as the conditions prescribed by the letter of the treaty are fulfilled. States would accept these obligations through ratification of the Convention establishing the agency, or by their adhesion, that is, by becoming a member of the system. Implementation of the control mechanism would be envisaged in the case of international conflicts only. An extension of such automatism to the field of non-international conflicts would probably not be acceptable to States and would therefore be unadvisable. Provision could be made for such circumstances, however, by the inclusion of an optional clause which would enable Member States and parties to the Convention to accept in advance the competence of the agency upon ratification or adhesion. A situation of this kind would be binding upon legal governments and insurgents alike, should the country in question be in the throes of a civil war. Equity dictates that a declaration of this kind during the course of an internal conflict be subordinated (as far as its effects are concerned) to the consent of the two parties—that is, the government and the insurgents.

It remains for us to make one last remark on 'international conflicts'. We have made use of the term without making a distinction between 'inter-state' conflicts and conflicts referred to in sub-paragraph 4 of Article 1 of Protocol I. We have done so intentionally since, in our opinion, general international law—at least, since the adoption of the Declaration on Principles of International Law concerning Friendly Relations and Co-operation among States in accordance with the Charter of the United Nations (Resolution 2625 (XXV) of the General Assembly)—considers conflicts between States and peoples fighting for their right to self-determination to be 'international conflicts'. Protocol I, therefore, is merely the confirmation of a legal conviction which existed prior to its adoption. Indeed, without this factor the acceptance of the provision in question in the Protocol would be unthinkable. States not having acceded to the Protocol are obviously not obliged to apply all the provisions contained therein to such conflicts. They are obliged, however, to apply the Geneva Conventions, because such conflicts are referred to by contemporary international law as international conflicts. By the same token, an 'internal' conflict which entails any form of intervention by foreign power(s) automatically leads to the application of the Geneva Conventions. This is because, from the point of view of the application of humanitarian law, the conflict in question must also be treated as an international conflict. Thus, all that is said of international conflicts is fully applicable to this kind of conflict, considered by some as 'mixed' conflicts.

Notes

1. ICJ Manual 1970.
2. Report of the International Law Commission, XXVI Session, 1976, General Assembly, Off. doc. A/31/10.
3. Pictet, Commentary, I.

Humanitarian Norms and Human Rights

Igor P Blishchenko

Contents

Igor Blishchenko is Professor of Legal Sciences and Chairman of International Law at the People's Friendship University Patrice Lumumba, Moscow. He attended the Conference of Government Experts on the Reaffirmation and Development of Humanitarian Law applicable in Armed Conflicts, Geneva, 1971-1972. He was a member of the Soviet Delegation at the first two sessions of the Diplomatic Conference on the Reaffirmation and Development of International Humanitarian Law.

It has been considered by several representatives of the doctrine that international humanitarian law comprises of a considerable number of norms forming the laws and customs of war which are directed, in particular, towards the protection of human rights and freedoms. In his work entitled 'The principles of international humanitarian law',[1] Professor Jean Pictet, former Vice-President of the ICRC, considers that international law comprises two branches—the first concerning the conduct of war, the second being the norms for the protection of human rights. He then sub-divides the laws of war into the Law of the Hague and the Law of Geneva, which together constitute humanitarian law.

We consider this system to be well-founded. In our opinion, it is possible to consider humanitarian law as a distinct branch of contemporary international law. In the literature, this branch of international law is also referred to as the 'international laws of armed conflict.'[2] These days, and in the light of the prohibition of war as a means of conducting foreign policy, the laws of war and the Law of the Hague should be excluded from this branch of international law as war is no longer licit by virtue of the prohibition of resorting to force contained in the Charter of the United Nations.

I Humanitarian law and international protection of human rights

As has been shown both by practice and by the works of the United Nations Human Rights Centre,[3] the essential problem in all situations of armed conflict is the international protection of human rights; in other words, the fundamental objective of what is known as the laws of war is the protection of human rights, both in time of peace and during periods of armed conflict. For this reason, it seems more appropriate to establish a closer relationship between the norms and principles which prohibit and limit the specific use of weapons, means and methods for the conduct of war on the one hand, and the international norms concerning human rights and freedoms which allow States to implement on their territory a regime of democracy and freedom on the other, thereby creating conditions which make it possible to exclude the eventuality of resorting to a war of aggression or to the means of massive destruction for the settlement of disputes.

Finally, mention should be made of the considerable number of principles and norms of international law aimed at limiting the arms race, and in particular, the principle of international law which calls for disarmament. This principle, which obliges States to observe and to implement agreements already concluded in the field of disarmament, should (in order to ensure the universality of such agreements in a spirit of good faith) enable the conclusion of new international agreements on arms limitations, real disarmament, the dismantling of the most dangerous types of mass-destruction weapons, and limits or bans on particularly harmful and dangerous weapons. In this way, complete and universal disarmament—including nuclear disarmament—would be possible under strict international control.

Clearly, respect for the norms of international humanitarian law in situations of international or non-international armed conflict depends on specific circumstances. We refer, in particular, to the Hague Conventions of 1889 and 1907, the Geneva Conventions of 1949 concerning the protection of victims of war and their additional Protocols of 1977, the Geneva Protocol of 1925, and the Convention for the banning and limitation of conventional weapons which cause additional harm and have disproportional effects. It may be said that the above-mentioned international instruments constitute conventional communities.

II—Jurisprudence as a source of humanitarian law

Jurisprudence, as a source of law, has a particular significance for international humanitarian law. Some may consider that jurisprudence does not constitute a source of law in international relations. Nevertheless, jurisprudence does influence the development of current international law; it enables us to determine whether a given norm is still valid or whether it has fallen into disuse.

1. The Nuremberg principles

In many cases, legal decisions have had, and continue to have, a strong influence on the formulation of both general principles and of the concrete norms of international law in a field—in this case, in the field of the laws and customs of war.[4] Accordingly, for example, the General Assembly of the United Nations confirmed in its Resolution of 11 December 1946 the principles of international law contained in the Charter of the Nuremberg Tribunal and their expression in the Tribunal's judgement. The resolution directed the Committee on the codification of international law to introduce this principle in the codification of offences against the peace and security of mankind and in international norms in general.[5]

At its Second session, the General Assembly directed the International Law Commission to formulate the principles of international law which were recognized by the Statutes of the Nuremberg Tribunal and which were expressed in its judgement, and to prepare a draft Code of Offences against the peace and security of mankind, indicating clearly the place to be accorded to the Nuremberg principles.[6] In 1954, the International Law Commission adopted the draft Code and submitted it for discussion at the General Assembly session. The General Assembly, however, decided to postpone discussions on the draft until such time as the definition of aggression was established.[7]

In other words, the United Nations had already considered the Nuremberg principles as being universally recognized. These principles, based on previously established norms of international law, contribute to the development of international law in the field of the laws and customs of war.

A comparison should be made between these norms and the Convention of 1949 on the Prevention and Punishment of the Crime of Genocide, according to which, genocide '. . . whether committed in time of peace or in time of war, is a crime under international law, which they (the Contracting Parties) undertake to prevent and to punish'. The Geneva Conventions of 1949 took into consideration the international penal responsibility of a whole series of war crimes which were not mentioned in the Hague Convention of 1907, but which for the first time were termed as such by the Statutes and judgement of the Nuremberg Tribunal. Furthermore, a series of resolutions by the General Assembly has termed the policy of apartheid and the deportation of local populations (such as that undertaken by the authorities of South Africa, Southern Rhodesia and Israel), as international crimes. These instruments bear undeniable witness to the influence of the principles contained in the decisions of the Nuremberg Tribunal.

In 1968 the General Assembly of the United Nations adopted

Non-Applicability of Statutory Limitations to the Convention on the War Crimes and Crimes against Humanity, which added to the number of crimes against humanity previously mentioned in the Charter of the Nuremberg Tribunal, in particular 'eviction by armed attack or occupation and inhuman acts resulting form the policy of apartheid, and the crime of genocide . . .'

The principles expressed in the Statutes of the Nuremberg Tribunal and in its judgement have had a strong influence on the development of the norms of international law concerning the extradition of war criminals. They have also strongly influenced the development of norms regarding the problem of the non-applicability of statutory limitations to these offences. Mention should also be made of the Resolution by the United Nations General Assembly, dated 13 February 1946 and entitled 'The extradition and punishment of war criminals', as well as of the Resolution by the General Assembly of the United Nations dated 31 October 1947 entitled 'Surrender of war criminals and traitors'. Both these Resolutions make reference to the obligation to extradite persons having committed the crimes mentioned in Article 6 of the Charter of the Nuremberg Tribunal (crimes against peace, war crimes, and crimes against humanity). Article I of the Declaration on Territorial Asylum, adopted by the General Assembly at its XXII Session in 1967, specifies 'The right to seek and enjoy asylum may not be invoked by any person with respect to whom there are serious reasons for considering that he has committed a crime against peace, a war crime or a crime against humanity . . .'[8]

In accordance with Article 1 of the Convention of 1968 on the Non-Applicability of Statutory Limitations to War Crimes, no statutory limitation shall apply to war crimes and crimes against humanity. Furthermore, in terms of Article 4 of the same Convention, States parties to the Convention are obliged to adopt any legislative or other measures necessary for the implementation of this stipulation.[9]

It may be concluded from the above, therefore, that legal decisions may have a sufficiently real influence on the development of international law, both with respect to its principles and to the direction of the development of norms of international law in a specific field.

2. Legal decisions

It may also be said that legal decisions in a given field have had, and continue to have, a strong influence on the application and development of international humanitarian law. We are already familiar with several international agreements and with several decisions by international organizations which contain principles and norms formulated in the wake of judgements of specific cases, made either by international legal authorities or by the legal authorities of individual States, and which serve to confirm or specify the various provisions contained in international humanitarian law in given situations.

It is from this standpoint that legal decisions should be included among the principal or subsidiary sources of international humanitarian law, since they play an important role in the formulation and development of this branch of law. Legal decisions serve to corroborate the existence of a norm of international law. They specify and confirm the law in a given situation, thereby influencing its development and fulfilment by means of inter-governmental agreements.

III The right to life in peaceful conditions

1. Disarmament

The human right to life, combined with the obligation of Member States of the international community to ensure and guarantee the full and free development of mankind in peaceful conditions, forms the very axis of the system of international humanitarian law. From this standpoint in particular, an essential relationship exists between this right and human rights.

In his speech before the June 1983 session of the Plenum of the Central Committee of the Soviet Communist Party, the Secretary-General, I.V. Andropov, said

'The threat posed by nuclear war against peace prompts us to reappraise the essential meaning of all communist movements. Communists have always struggled against the domination and exploitation of man by man; and today, they continue their struggle for the protection of human civilization, for the human right to life'.[10]

What exactly does this human right to life entail? The human right to life essentially comprises the following elements, a combination of which constitutes an international law obligation: disarmament, peace among Nations, protection of the environment and of mankind, and co-operation between States with respect to global problems of the development of mankind.

All these elements have found expression in the most essential instrument for contemporary relations   the Charter of the United Nations—and in a whole series of international agreements. In its Decree on Peace, and its Declaration on the Rights of Workers and Exploited Peoples, the Soviet State confirmed the convergence of socialism, peace and respect for human rights as follows: 'The suppression of all exploitation of man by man, the revolutionary struggle for the "democratic peace" of Nations, and respect for the "free self-determination of Nations" are essential objectives of the Soviet Socialist government.' These principles still form the basis of the Soviet Union's foreign policy.[11]

An analysis of the instruments of international law serves to highlight one international obligation in particular: it is the duty of governments to ensure peace in close collaboration with the measures to be taken by States for the implementation of human rights and freedoms. These days, the right to life cannot be considered to be merely the right to remain alive; the right to life entails the development of man in society under peaceful conditions. This close interdependence between the obligation of States to maintain peace and security among Nations on the one hand, and human rights and freedoms on the other, constitutes the obligation to attain economic and social progress. Indeed, this interdependence serves to exemplify the attitude of the Soviet government towards the essential problems of international relations. This attitude is expressed through active participation in the preparation of the essential instruments of international law in the field of human rights and freedoms.

It may be recalled that, in the 'Preamble to the Charter' of the United Nations, the peoples again reaffirmed their faith in fundamental human rights in particular, and resolved to promote social progress and better standards of life in larger freedom, and to unite their strength to maintain international peace and security. These issues are referred to in Article 1 of the Charter, which enumerates the purposes of the United Nations, and again in Article 55, which deals with international economic and social coperation. The fundamental relationship between maintaining peace and attaining the protection of human rights is, once again, confirmed in the first sub-paragraph of the Preamble to the Universal Declaration of Human Rights, and in the two International Covenants on Human Rights, as follows: '. . . recognition of the inherent dignity and of the equal and inalienable rights of all members of the human family is the foundation of freedom, justice and peace in the world'. Likewise, the preamble to the Proclamation by the International Conference on Human Rights at Teheran in 1968 recognizes that 'Peace is the universal aspiration of mankind' and that 'peace and justice are indispensable to the full realization of human rights and fundamental freedoms'.

Over the last few years, publications emanating from the international organizations bear witness to a justified trend in which peace is considered on a wider, universally acceptable basis. It should be stressed that this attitude, the formulation of which has been influenced by the efforts for peace made by the socialist countries and other peace-loving nations, is opposed to, and stands out against, the attitude adopted by the Western countries. The right to life is only considered by Western countries in an abstract fashion, thereby alienating it from the context of protection and its implementation. Western publications, and publications on the relationship between peace and development in particular, fail to stress one of the most important conditions of the right to life and one which guarantees peace and development—that of disarmament.[12] When we speak of the right to life as a human right, or as a principle of international law, it is essential that, first and foremost, disarmament be identified as an essential condition thereto, as well as the guarantee of the protection of this right. In other words, a solution to the disarmament problem consititutes the most important condition for development and the protection of human rights. Conversely, the implementation and guarantees of essential human rights and freedoms are obviously the fundamental elements of the struggle for disarmament and the protection of the right to life. During the debates at the XXIII Session of the Human Rights Commission, the participants expressed their conviction that total and universal disarmament, combined with a halt to the arms race, were two essential conditions for the protection of human rights.[13]

2. Co-operation among States in the field of development

During the United Nations Seminar held in Geneva in 1980 on the influence of the persistence of an unjust international economic order on the economies of the developing countries, and on the dangers to fundamental human rights and freedoms caused by this persistence, it was stressed that the arms race also represents a danger for development, and that vast sums of money are spent on arms while millions of people still live in abject poverty. Disarmament would seem to be a prerequisite to the full protection of the right to peace and the right to development. During the course of the debates at this Seminar, emphasis was placed on the essential relationship between the attainment of the right to peace, respect for human rights and the implementation of the right to development. In this context, the total disarmament objective plays an important role.[14]

Over the past few years, Western literature[15] and the documents emanating from the UN organs[16] have made increasing use of the expression 'right to development'. The various authors concerned, however, all have a different understanding of the meaning of this expression. During the 1960s, the word 'development' was understood to mean economic development alone. Since the late 1960s and early 1970s, however, the term has been interpreted as meaning economic development undertaken with due respect for human rights, in that respect of this kind complements social and cultural development. Although, during the former period, the right to development devolved upon nations and States, nowadays one speaks of the right of individuals to development, and of the human right to development.

3. The right of peoples to self-determination

The 'Declaration on Principles of International Law concerning Friendly Relations and Cooperation among States in accordance with the Charter of the United Nations' (2625 (XXV)) states, in particular, that all nations have the right to choose their destiny, without any form of interference; that they have the right to determine their political status and to pursue their economic, social and cultural development; and that every State has the duty to respect these rights in accordance with the provisions of the Charter. Furthermore, the principle of self-determination makes particular provision for the obligation of each Member State of the international community to take steps which ensure universal respect for, and the promotion of, the implementation of fundamental human rights and freedoms, in accordance with the Charter of the United Nations. In our opinion, it would be incorrect to limit the right to development, the right of nations and peoples to self-determination, merely to issues concerning 'the protection of health, food, shelter, work and working conditions, social security, the right to leisure and individual freedoms', as was done during the discussions in the Human Rights Commission.[17] It seems to us that this right should be taken in a much broader context and, as such, takes the form of a fundamental principle of contemporary international law and international relations. It has already been enshrined in a number of fundamental instruments of the international community, such as the Charter of the United Nations, the Universal Declaration of Human Rights, the International Covenants on Human Rights, and various UN Declarations and Conventions on the subject.

In particular, the Declaration on the Establishment of a New international Economic Order of 1974 states that an order of this kind should be founded on full respect for the principle of self-determination for all nations; and on the right of each country to choose the economic and social system considered by it to be the most suitable for its own developmental needs, and without any form of discrimination. Furthermore, the Order should be based on the absolute sovereignty of each State with regard to its natural resources and economic activities. [18]

The right of nations and peoples to self-determination necessarily presupposes the obligation of co-operation among States and peoples in creating conditions for the broadest and most complete fulfilment of this right. Yet, this obligation in no way disregards or modifies the existing system of principles and norms of contemporary international law; the more complete its fulfilment, the more effective the obligation will be—provided that other norms and principles for the respect of sovereignty and non-interference in internal affairs are observed. The efforts made by members of the international community for the implementation of the right to development of the Palestinian Arab nation, including the right to the establishment of the Palestinian State, as well as the efforts made by States in aid of peoples subjected to colonial domination, may serve as examples in this regard. Nicaragua, Kampuchea, Afghanistan, India, Ethiopia, Nigeria and others, may also serve as examples in this respect.

The obligation to co-operate which exists in international law stems so much from the universally accepted principles of international law—partly the right of nations and peoples to self-determination—that it constitutes an independent principle of international law in its own right. This principle is applicable to all fields of international relations and is not merely limited to the field of economic relations. The principle of co-operation among States, formulated in the Declaration on Principles of International Law concerning Friendly Relations and Co-operations among States in accordance with the Charter of the United Nations, is thus extended to encompass the economic, social, cultural and technical fields, and to include the field of trade relations, in accordance with the principle of sovereign equality and non-interference. Co-operation of this kind will ensure the protection of peace and international security as being the most important conditions for the universal respect for, and the implementation of, human rights and fundamental freedoms for all, and for the elimination of all forms of racial discrimination and religious intolerance, especially in the case of the developing countries.

If the above is borne in mind, then the opinion that the right to development implies the generalization of means and 'the synthesis of the greatest number of human rights' [19] may be deemed to be correct. Yet this right should not be limited to human economic and social rights alone. As is seen in practice, human rights, formulated and regulated by international agreements contribute substantially to the development of human rights as proclaimed by the international community and protected by the organization of the political and legal system of the State. From this standpoint, the attenuation of all difficulties in international relations which thwart the effective co-operation of States in all areas of socio-economic development is an important prerequisite to the widest possible attainment of the rights of each individual, especially in the case of the developing countries.

At this juncture, we should specify which human rights we are referring to. Firstly, it should be stated that one group of human rights should not be arbitrarily separated from another, let alone opposed to another. 'Human rights cannot be considered from the perspective of distinct elements to be distributed in a given order according to the significance attributed to them. By their very nature, these rights represent an indivisible entity and reflect the fundamental oneness of the entity of mankind.'[20]

This is precisely the attitude adopted by the Soviet State during the preparation of the Covenant on human rights and freedoms, when it was decided that one Covenant should cover economic, social and cultural rights. The socialist concept of human rights and freedoms stems from the fact that the recognition and protection of economic, social and cultural human rights enables mankind to enjoy his civil and political rights to the fullest extent possible, and thus to make a real contribution to the development of society. It is precisely from this perspective that we consider the human right to life, which attributes a unique value to mankind himself. The defence of this value under present circumstances, faced with the threat of the arms race pursued by imperialism and by the danger of a nuclear catastrophe, is the concern of all mankind.

The authors of the socialist countries,[21] as well as the legislative practice of these countries, have always stressed that in a socialist society human rights are not, cannot be, limited to economic rights and material well-being alone. Political rights are conceived 'not as autonomous abstract values', but essentially in a functional manner, that is, as the means whereby the large masses of workers are assured the right to participate in the government and whereby the democratic nature of the State and the development of society are guaranteed.

It is for this reason that, considering the importance attributed to the economic, social and cultural aspects of human rights, and considering the formulation of the concept of these rights as an essential element for mankind and society, the development of society in the socialist countries still signifies that civil and political human rights are proclaimed, implemented and developed in peaceful conditions.

We support the important declaration contained in the Report by the Secretary-General of the United Nations, which states that any strategy for development which is founded on political repression and on violations of human rights, even though it may be effective from the point of view of fulfilling specific economic objectives, cannot lead to real development,[22] because it inexorably leads to the violation of peace, to aggression, and to the appropriation of another's territory. It should be emphasized at this point that the affirmation of the protection of human rights and freedoms, within the context of human rights as contained in the Conventions and international agreements prepared within the framework of the United Nations in particular, constitutes an important condition for development and forms an integral part of the strategy of development. It should also be noted that the human rights concept, as formulated by contemporary international law, is oriented towards development and is opposed to violence, domination, and to improper use of the law to the detriment of development.

4. Solidarity and interdependence of States

In our era, the right to life does not merely signify peace under conditions of development; it also signifies the cooperation of States with regard to the global problems facing mankind today, on the solution of which life on earth depends. This leads us to conclude that the efforts of all States must inevitably be united if the global problems which thwart the development of mankind are to be solved. Examples of such global problems are: primarily, the disarmament problem, but also problems concerning the protection of the environment, disease control, raw materials, energy, food, and the peaceful exploitation of the oceans. These problems must be solved for mankind as a whole, which again leads us to the question of co-operation among States for the resolution of the problems of the new international economic order. It must be emphasized that the solution of these global problems is closely linked to the recognition of the importance and value of the individual, and to the international community's responsibility for 'the social destiny of mankind'.

Combined efforts alone, based on the principle of not being prejudicial to the development of any Member State of the international community, will lead to the solution of these global problems in the interest of all peoples and every individual. Furthermore, co-operation of this kind may have, and does have, a positive effect on the process of peaceful development. From this standpoint, the elimination of the arms race serves to reinforce peace among nations and to liberate the means and resources for solving other global problems, thereby attaining the result referred to in Article 25 of the Universal Declaration of Human Rights, that is, that everyone 'has the right to a standard of living adequate for the health and well-being of himself and of his family...'

Development is a progressive objective, peculiar to every society, every nation, and every individual. The right to life in peaceful conditions and the right to development are an integral part of the right of nations and peoples to self-determination, the attainment of which is an obligation of all States.

It is difficult to agree with the conclusions that the right to development, the right to peace, the right to health and the right to a balanced economic environment alone form the fundamentals of the concept of solidarity and interdependence among nations.[23] It should be stressed that all human rights and freedom are based on solidarity and interdependence, so that each incidence of improper use of certain human rights inevitably leads to the non-respect of other rights of another individual.

IV Conclusions

In our opinion, therefore, international humanitarian law comprises two parts: the applicable international norms which constitute the regime of human rights and freedoms in times of armed conflict; and the applicable norms which concern the arms race limitation regime, serve to limit and prohibit the elaboration of new weapons, and which concern disarmament.

In other words, the human right to life forms the basis of the current system of international humanitarian law; it is guaranteed by the application of all principles and norms of international contemporary law and, more immediately, by the application of all the above-mentioned sources for the regulation of international law with regard to co-operation among States in humanitarian issues. Clearly, the implementation of international humanitarian law must be effected in accordance with the norms and fundamental principles of international contemporary law and, above all, in accordance with the Charter of the United Nations.

Notes

1. J. Pictet: The principles of international humanitarian law, Geneva, 1966; see also, by the same author: Humanitarian Law and the Protection

of Victims of War, Geneva, 1973.

2. Cf, A.I. Potorak, L.I. Savinski: Armed conflict and as law, Moscow, 1978; D.B. Levin: Current problems in the theory of international law, Moscow, 1974; I.N. Arouibasov: International law, Moscow, 1980. The Law of Armed Conflicts N. 9 1971, p.5.

3. Cf, for example, Ya. A. Ostrovski: The United Nations and the protection of human rights. IZD-VO IMO, 1968; J. Blishchenko: Die Definierung des humanitren Vlkerrechts, Festschrift fr Friedrich Berber, Mnchen, 1973.

4. See I.P. Blishchenko, Precedents in international law, Moscow, 1977.

5. General Assembly, Resolution 95 (I)

6. General Assembly, Resolution 177 (II)

7. General Assembly, Resolution 877 (IX)

8. General Assembly, Resolution 2312 (XXII)

9. General Assembly, Resolution 2391 (XXIII)

10. See Pravda, 16 June 1983

11. See I.P. Blischenko, A.P. Glebov, Konstitucia SR, Vnechnei Politike Sovetskogo Gosudarstva, Moscow, 1978.

12. See, for example, J.-M. Domenach: Aid for development, a moral obligation? Edited for the *NNJ Centre of economic and social information*, 1971, p. 141. ('Furthermore, the establishment of peace does not merely mean the attainment of political conditions within which governments may conclude trade agreements: the underlying meaning is the attainment of structures and the preparation of methods which enable States, and the least-developed States in particular, to make full use of their natural resources with the help of other States. Consequently, peace does not stem from a negative need, that is, the need for the absence of war; rather, it is the consequence of a positive need arising from the converging goals of various States, each of which strives for development along its own lines'). Lester B. Pearson (1968) in 'Reshaping the international order', Report to the Club of Rome, coordinated by J. Timbergen, 1977, p. 59. ('Peace, coexistence and the dignity of all individuals'). Expert meeting on human rights, human needs and the establishment of a new international economic order (UNESCO), SS.78/CONF. 630/12, pp. 83-90.

13. E/CH, 4/CP, 1978, item 39.

14. ST/HR/SER, items 88, 89, 107, 132.

15. See, for example, W. Rostow: The stages of economic growth. Cambridge University Press, 1971; D. Morawetz: Twenty-five years of economic development, 1950-1975, Washington, 1977.

16. See E/CH. 4/1334.

17. See E/1979/36: E/CN.4 /1347, p.26

18. General Assembly, Resolution 3201 (S/VI, 1.5.1974). See F. Rigaux:

The right of peoples to self-determination and to permanent sovereignty over resources, in the context of the establishment of a new international economic order (Doc. 4/UNESCO-SS-78 (CONF. 630/5)). See H. Gros Espiell: The implementation of the United Nations resolution concerning the right to self-determination of peoples subjected to colonial and foreign domination (E/CN, 4/Sub. 2/405, n.139, 45). See also E/CN, 4/Sub. 2/404).

19. E/CN. 4/1334, p. 36; J. Rivero: On the right to development (Doc. SS-178 (CONF. 630/2)); H. Gros Espiell: The right to development as a right of the individual (Doc. SS-78/CONF. 630).

20. See Th.C. van Boven: Partners in the Promotion and Protection of Human Rights, Netherlands International Law Review, v. 24, 1/2 (1977), p. 387.

21. See for example J. Simoniedes Wklad Polski w ksztaltomanie miedzynarodnpmego model praw cztomieka, Sprawky miedzynarodowe, 1977 N. 10, p. 19, 21. A. Michalska, Podstawowe prawa czlowieka w prawie wewnetrznym a Pakty Praw czlowieka, Warsaw, 1976, p.37. W. Skrzydlo, O prawaxh politycznych obywateli PRY, Nowe Drogi, 1976, N. 10. Socialist concept of Human Rights, Budapest, 1965. J. Grospic, J. Wlanoz, Koncepee lidskich a abvanskich praw od Vekeno Rijna po soucast nost, Pravnik, 1977. J. Ruczynski, Menschen Rechte und Klassenrechte, Berlin, 1978. V.M. Tschikvadse, Socialism and human rights; Leninist ideas and the contemporary era, Moscow, 1979.

22. E/CN. 4/1334, p. 74

23. Expert meeting on human rights, Human Needs and the Establishment of a New International Economic Order (UNESCO), SS 78/CONF.630/12, pp. 90-93.

The Socialist Countries and the Laws of Armed Conflict

Jiri Toman

Contents

Jiri Toman is the Deputy Director of the Henry Dunant Institute in Geneva. He is the author of numerous works in the field of humanitarian law. He co-authored 'The Laws of Armed Conflicts: A Collection of Conventions, Resolutions and other Documents' (Schindler-Toman, 1973, 1981), and 'The Spirit of Uppsala', proceedings of the Joint UNITAR/Uppsala University Seminar on International Law and Organization for a New World Order (1984). He is the editor of the 'Index of the Geneva Conventions' (1973). The opinions expressed in this article are solely those of the author.

e) Conference of High Contracting Parties
f) The Enquiry Commission
g) The International Fact-Finding Commission
h) Reprisals
i) Repression of violations and the superior order

III—Conclusions

I Soviet doctrine with regard to the laws of armed conflicts: terminology

The Soviet doctrine of international law prefers the usage of the traditional term 'the laws of armed conflict' as opposed to 'international humanitarian law'. The former is a more accurate definition of the subject, i.e. regulations governing international and non-international armed conflicts. The term 'international humanitarian law' only appeared very recently, specifically since the Diplomatic Conference on the Reaffirmation and Development of International Humanitarian Law applicable in Armed Conflicts (particularly in works by Khlestov, Blishchenko, Herczegh and Mencer). Frequent use is also made of the term 'laws and customs of war'.

The laws of armed conflict were recently defined in a Soviet manual

as an ensemble of the principles and (conventional or customary) norms which govern the process of struggle in armed conflicts of an international or internal nature from the onset of the conflict until its conclusion. This law determines the status, rights and obligations of the parties to the armed conflict, their mutual relations, and their relations with neutral States; they regulate the use of violence during the course of the armed conflict (with regard to its duration, spacing, persons, objectives and means); they protect victims of war and civilian objects in the face of direct military violence; and determine responsibility for war crimes. Their objective, in accordance with the laws of humanity and the dictates of the public conscience, is to decrease to the minimum the sufferings caused by armed struggle and to extend the application of the principles of humanity in the case of armed conflicts.[1]

1. Law of Geneva, law of The Hague

Poltorak and Savinskii, the authors of this definition, refute the subdivision of the law into the law of The Hague and the law of Geneva. In their view, this subdivision constitutes a threat aimed at undermining the humanitarian aspect of the laws of armed conflict as a whole. According to the Soviet authors, the subdivision contradicts the very content of the norms which regulate the conduct of armed struggle, because none of these norms permits belligerents to wage war in an inhumane fashion. Humanitarian considerations apply to the laws of armed conflict as a whole—both to the law of The Hague and to the law of Geneva.

2. Principles of humanity and military necessity

The Soviet doctrine on international law attaches great importance to the definition of the principles of international law and, similarly, to the laws of armed conflict. According to Poltorak and Savinskii, the elaboration of these principles would make provision for 'not only the confirmation of existing norms, but also more precision, clarification, and a better definition' of these norms.

As is known, the laws of armed conflict are governed by two fundamental principles: that of humanity and that of military necessity. According to Marxist philosophy, there are fundamental differences between the 'principle of humanity' in bourgeois society and that in socialist society. Marxism—in the minds of these two authors—places the humanitarian concept on a higher level, having as its objective 'the creation of conditions for the free and harmonious development of mankind' in order to assure 'the promotion of economic, political and moral structures' and 'the construction of a stable peace between peoples, the progressive development of humanity as a whole'. According to the socialist system, as far as the belligerent parties are concerned, there is no possible contradiction between the superior principle of humanity and the raisons d'Etat known as 'military necessity'. For the military necessity of a socialist State inevitably serves the higher interest of humanity. Thus, this equality of interests excludes all possibility of contradiction.

Military necessity, as applied by the Soviets, will always be an expression of humanity at its higher level—collective. In this context, therefore, the principle of humanity expresses both the needs of humanity and of public order.

Soviet doctrine affirms that 'if the objective of a war is just and progressive, the classes and States waging that war cannot be indifferent to the methods and means by which such an objective is attained. It is from this viewpoint that the principle of a just war repudiates senseless ferocity and violent acts which are not dictated by military necessity.'

Furthermore, Soviet doctrine reaffirms that reference to military necessity is only possible in exceptional cases and only where it is provided for by the specific norms of the laws of armed conflict. These norms, such as Article 28 of Geneva Convention II of 1949, set forth specific obligations for the party referring to military necessity.

The exception of military necessity is only possible in cases 'where material, cultural and other values are in exceptional danger, but not in cases where such a decision may affect the lives, health or honour of mankind, that is, human values. This tendency corresponds entirely to the principle of the protection of human rights, proclaimed by contemporary international law, and is of the utmost significance in the case of armed conflicts'.

According to the Soviet authors, therefore, the fundamental principle in the sphere of armed struggle is the principle of humanization. All other principles are merely deductions of this principle or its concretization.

Thus, the Soviet authors affirm the existence of the following principles in particular:

* the principle of inadmissibility of the use of barbaric and inhumane means during the course of armed struggle;
* the principle of the protection of victims of war and civilian objects;
* the principle of equal treatment for belligerents and the prohibition of discrimination;
* the principle of honour and good faith in the choice of methods used during the course of military operations;
* the principle of responsibility of belligerents for war crimes.

Each of the above-mentioned principles is developed upon in Soviet doctrine and could serve a useful purpose in the search for a common basis for the establishment of the principles of the laws of armed conflict. This would undeniably contribute towards a deeper understanding and a better application of these laws.

3. 'Jus ad bellum', 'jus in bello'

The prohibition of war by the Charter of the United Nations has prompted many Soviet authors, such as Korovin, to stress the difference between the rights of the aggressor and the rights of the victim of aggression.

More recently, however, numerous Soviet authors, notably Poltorak and Savinskii, have refuted this approach and recognize the need to distinguish between 'jus ad bellum' and 'jus in bello'. They affirm, and rightly so, that if regulations governing the laws of warfare are to be applied in a discriminatory fashion to one party and not the other, it is highly unlikely that these regulations will ever be respected.

Nevertheless, this does not mean that they recognize complete equality between the aggressor and the victim of aggression. This question reappeared during the Diplomatic Conference of 1974-1977 and was subsequently incorporated into the final text of the Preamble to Protocol I in the form of a paragraph which recalls the duty of every State to refrain in its international relations from the threat or use of force.

II Attitudes of the socialist countries at the Diplomatic Conference of 1974-1977, and their suggestions

The role played by the USSR at the conference on the codification of the laws of armed conflict has been an active one. On the eve of the Diplomatic Conference of 1974-1977, the Soviet Union expressed its faith in the Geneva Conventions and its determination to maintain their validity. USSR representatives and Soviet internationalists alike, however, pointed out that certain lacunae would have to be considered during the Conference itself.

1. Lacunae in the laws of armed conflict and the extension of existing regulations

The Soviet authors noted the need to improve the protection of civilian populations, to develop regulations concerning the methods and means of combat, and to improve on the provisions governing non-international armed conflict.

In addition to these lacunae, some situations require greater precision and extension of the current regulations. This is particularly applicable to the definition of irregular forces, the development of regulations for maritime warfare, submarine warfare, military contraband, the arming of commercial ships, etc.

a) Obsolete provisions: The laws of armed conflict also include provisions which have become obsolete owing to developments in international relations or other branches of international law. This point has been raised by Soviet authors with respect to Article 36 of the Regulation of The Hague of 1907 concerning the resumption of hostilities, which is inconsistent with the prohibition of threat and the use of force.

These issues were at the centre of the debates at the 1974-1977 Conference, and moderately satisfactory solutions were found in some cases. Other questions remain pending as the international community has yet to find solutions acceptable to all or the majority. The next codification phase will, therefore, have to be awaited before solutions can be found for these issues.

At this stage, the socialist group's homogeneity and their unanimity should be recalled. Thoroughly prepared before and during each session of the Conference, this tactic enabled the socialist States to take advantage of contradictions occurring among other groups, such as the Western countries group or the Third World countries group.

For example, the Western group's refusal to take political realities into account, combined with their lack of flexibility vis--vis the problems of wars of national liberation, prompted the Third World countries to accept a restrictive definition of these wars in order to obtain the two-thirds majority necessary for the adoption of their amendment on this issue. This move was favourable to the Socialist countries since it excluded the possibility of applying paragraph 4 of Article 1 against their political interests, particularly within the USSR and the community of socialist countries. The same applied to the articles concerning combatant status and the definition of mercenaries. But it would be wrong to assume that the socialist and Third World countries were party to the same interests, or that the Soviet Union was acting 'on behalf of progress'. The position adopted by the socialist countries conformed entirely to both their domestic and their international political interests. Furthermore, so long as these interests so required, the Soviet Union and the socialist bloc willingly joined forces with the 'imperialist powers' in order to thwart the wishes of the Afro-Asian and Latin American countries.

This would explain the move made by the developed countries against the developing countries over provisions concerning the methods and means of combat, where a very limited progress had nontheless been obtained. The same applied to the Ad hoc Committee on Conventional Weapons, especially with respect to draft Article 86(a). In this case, the two groups were so sharply divided that, for various reasons, the countries of both East and West prevented progress in the establishment of a more effective control mechanism or the adoption of the article on the superior order.

2. Definition of international and non-international armed conflict

During the preparation of Article 3 common to the Geneva Conventions of 12 August 1949 concerning 'conflicts not of an international character', the Soviet Union proved to be the strongest supporter of the automatic application of all the Conventions to such conflicts. The Soviet doctrine considered Article 3 to be a norm of 'jus cogens' and pronounced itself 'de lege feranda' for more detailed regulations concerning non-international conflicts, especially with respect to the status of combatants, the treatment of prisoners, the protection of civilian populations and the prohibition of reprisals.

During the Diplomatic Conference of 1974-1977 and the expert meetings which preceded it, the socialist countries proved to be considerably more restrictive. Firstly, the USSR showed little interest in the regulation of internal conflicts and considered the issue to be one of little urgency. During the Conferences of Governmental Experts, the Soviet Union displayed a clear reluctance towards the extension of international protection or a broader definition of internal conflict. After the adoption of paragraph 4 of Article 1 of Protocol I, the Soviet Union was in a position where it could easily give the impression of supporting a protocol on non-international conflicts without there being the slightest risk to USSR interests.

During the course of the discussions, the socialist countries supported a restrictive definition of non-international armed conflict which combined both objective and subjective elements and allowed the Party on whose territory the conflict takes place to recognize or not to recognize the existence of the conflict. Since the choice of a high threshold for the conflict only concerns conflicts of major intensity, the socialist countries could afford to be more generous with respect to the level of protection and a clearer definition of such protection.

During the expert meetings and the Diplomatic Conference of 1974-1977 itself, the socialist countries adopted the following positions in particular:

* retaining the term 'non-international armed conflict';
* distinction between guerilla and non-international armed conflict
* the adoption of two separate protocols, including a separate protocol on non-international armed conflicts (contrary to their posture at the 1949 Diplomatic Conference at Geneva, where the socialist countries supported the application of all the Conventions to both types of conflict);
* prohibition of the means and methods of combat, without specifically prohibiting weapons, but based on the principle of distinguishing between military objects and protected persons and objects, and prohibiting the destruction of the natural conditions of the human   environment;
* extending the protection of victims and care of the sick and wounded, prohibiting the use of torture and breaches against the individual;
* cautions against the attempts to extend the cases of application;
* opposition to the creation of a new type of conflict, such as a mixed conflict, since all parties are acting illicitly;
* doubts concerning the possibility of making distinctions between internal conflicts according to the degree of organization of the rebel party;
* relations between the authorities in power and the insurgents, governed by domestic penal law and fundamental guarantees.

The socialist countries were opposed both to the intervention of any international body in the legal definition of armed conflict and to any procedure allowing for an objective ascertainment of the existence of a conflict. It appears to us that the socialist countries were willing, if need be, to accept the competence of the Security Council in this regard, since the right to veto enables them to retain the subjective evaluation of each situation.

They also had a restrictive attitude vis-à-vis any control organism having the right to automatic intervention in a conflict without the express authorization of the State concerned. They prefer to maintain the present state of the right of initiative of the ICRC which depends entirely on the authorization of the State concerned. They also have a negative attitude towards the creation of an institution of impartial observers.

The socialist countries favoured exclusion of the application of Protocol II, and even of Article 3, in situations of internal disturbances and tensions on the grounds of the principle of non-intervention in the domestic affairs and sovereignty of the State. The State must be allowed to maintain the complete right of appreciation with regard to the measures to be taken to repress a riot or an insurrection in accordance with the law.

The socialist countries do not admit the difference between the fields of application of Article 3 and Protocol II. According to Mr. Graefrath, a distinction of this kind has an important political bearing and 'the introduction of new categories and difficult distinctions was not calculated to strengthen the development of international humanitarian law. Instead, it might encourage interference in the internal affairs of States.'

Bearing in mind the above, it is highly unlikely that the socialist countries would support any project for the establishment of regulations or the proclamation of humanitarian principles in the case of internal disturbances and tensions. An attempt of this nature was made by the proposal for a 'Declaration of fundamental rights of the individual in time of internal disturbances or public emergency'. Although most of the experts at the Conference of Government Experts were opposed to this initiative, some expressed the wish that the ICRC pursue the issue. Likewise, the Independent Commission could study the matter and pave the way for a declaration of this nature in the not too distant future, taking into account the ever-increasing tendency of human rights bodies to promote the better protection of mankind in exceptional situations.

a) Protection of civilian populations and civilian objects: The socialist countries also proved to be very active with respect to the protection of victims of international armed conflicts, and numerous proposals in this regard were included in the final text of Protocol I. The socialist countries favoured greater protection of the wounded, sick and shipwrecked, and of prisoners of war.

In particular, they made a number of suggestions concerning the protection of civilian populations and civilian objects, although their wishes were not always entirely satisfied in this regard.

b) Protection of cultural objects The Additional Protocols also contain a provision concerning the protection of cultural objects, applied without prejudice to the provisions of the Hague Convention of 1954. In the periodic reports addressed to UNESCO on the application of this Convention, Poland in particular suggested that revisions be made concerning the reservation of military necessity and that provisions contained in the Hague Protocol of 1954 be incorporated into the Convention in the form of a chapter on restitutions and, if need be, on reparations. They also stressed the need to pass legislation on breaches and sanctions.

c) Mercenaries: The socialist countries supported the article concerning mercenaries, although in their opinion the article 'would have been more satisfactory if it had also dealt with aspects such as the establishment of responsibility of States which authorize or encourage the recruitment, training or employment of mercenaries'. On the other hand, they made no mention of hidden forms of mercenary activities, which constitute a similar danger. The prohibition of mercenary activities should be accompanied by a guarantee of non-interference in order to avoid the emergence of new types of mercenary activities stemming from political interference in the internal affairs of States.

d) Mechanisms of scrutiny used for the application of international humanitarian law: Prior to the Diplomatic Conference of 1974-1977 the socialist countries wished to retain the existing mechanisms of scrutiny for the application of international humanitarian law and, in particular, the strict application of the principles contained in the Geneva Conventions of 1949. The consent of the Parties is considered to be an indispensable condition for the designation of the Protecting Power or its substitute. In the socialist countries' view, any automatism in the designation process is incompatible with the reality of international relations and with the principle of sovereignty.

Article 5, paragraph 2 of Draft Protocol I introduced a new form of designation of the Protecting Power through the good offices of the ICRC. This proposal was supported by numerous countries. Modified and restricted by its reference to the consent of the Parties concerned, the proposal was subsequently incorporated into the amendment introduced by the Soviet Socialist Byelorussian Republic, the Ukrainian Soviet Socialist Republic and the USSR on this subject.

In cases where, despite the adoption of these procedures, no Protecting Power is designated, experts from the Democratic Republic of Germany proposed the introduction of a time limit for the designation of a Protecting Power. According to the proposal, if no Protecting Power is designated within the time limit, the ICRC or any other humanitarian body would act as substitute on condition that the consent of the interested Parties is obtained.

The USSR delegate at the Conference considered that 'the activities of any humanitarian organization that might act as an intermediary would be of an extraordinary nature and it was therefore inappropriate to lay down an obligatory provision in the proposed provision'. He was rather in favour of maintaining the clause 'subject to the consent of the parties to the conflict'.

In draft Protocol I, the ICRC had proposed two alternatives for paragraph 3 of Article 5 concerning the designation of a substitute. According to the first alternative, the ICRC 'may assume the functions of a substitute... provided the Parties to the conflict agree and insofar as these functions are compatible with its own activities'. The second was a more automatic formula according to which 'the Parties to the conflict shall accept the offer made by the International Committee of the Red Cross, if it deems it necessary, to act as a substitute...' Although the Vice President of the ICRC reaffirmed that the ICRC 'had never dreamt of acting as substitute for the Protecting Powers without the consent of the Parties to the conflict', those countries supporting national sovereignty were strongly in favour of the former, more restrictive proposal which stresses the need for consent. This version obtained the final agreement of the delegations as expressed in Article 5, paragraph 4.

What is the attitude of the socialist countries in cases where replacement organizations may act as substitutes?

Once again, it must be stressed that no organization, in the view of the socialist countries, should have the automatic right of substitute. The socialist countries undeniably prefer the principle of consent to a 'system offering guarantees of security in case of dispute', thereby giving the Parties themselves complete freedom in the designation procedure. Furthermore, they do not wish to see the Parties' choice limited by giving any form of preference to one body over another. This primarily affects the ICRC, which is generally recognized as being the most likely humanitarian institution to act as a substitute.

Thus, the Soviet draft of paragraph 3 of Article 5 refers only to 'a humanitarian organization offering every guarantee of impartiality and efficacy' to act as substitute, without even mentioning the ICRC. Indeed, Mr. Rechetniak, delegate of the Ukrainian Soviet Socialist Republic even expressed the desire to 'expand the circle of organizations suitable for the role of substitute'.

In 1972, during the Conference of Government Experts, the Romanian experts suggested that, if need be, the United Nations Organization could designate the Protecting Power, on the condition that their choice was acceptable to the concerned Parties. The same proposal recurred in 1974 at the Diplomatic Conference. It appears that the Soviet delegation does not share this point of view and asks which organ of the United Nations would be responsible for designating the Protecting Power. The Delegation of the Democratic Republic of Germany was also opposed to the designation of a substitute by the UN, as proposed in Article 4(a). The other socialist countries were not very supportive of co-operation between the UN and the ICRC in the field of control, and Poland even preferred that complete freedom of action be left to the ICRC within the framework of the Geneva Conventions of 1949.

Norway and Egypt raised the question of the creation of a permanent organ within the UN system, which would not only act as Protecting Power in cases where no Protecting Power was designated or where this role was assumed by the ICRC, but would also assume responsibility for investigating and reporting violations of the Conventions. In its response to the ICRC questionnaire, Poland had already adopted a decidedly negative attitude. During the second Session of the Conference of Government Experts, experts from the socialist countries opposed the creation of a 'fall-back institution' and stressed, inter alia, the financial aspect of the issue. They also adopted this attitude during the Diplomatic Conference. Nor did the socialist countries favour the introduction of regional or other organizations in this regard.

e) Conference of High Contracting Parties: A draft submitted by 18 Third World countries (CDDH/I/75) provided for a last resort solution for cases where, despite the envisaged procedure, no Protecting Power can be designated. This last resort proposal entailed the designation of the Protecting Power by a Conference of High Contracting Parties.

Since the amendment entrusted decisions concerning designation to the Conference of High Contracting Parties without the consent of the interested Parties, the general attitude of the socialist countries was inevitably a negative one.

The text of Article 5, as adopted, is a fairly clear reflection of the classical concept of the role of the Protecting Power, as defined by the USSR and the other socialist countries over the past decades. The adopted text represents a step backward with respect to the Geneva Conventions of 1949, when the principle of designation of the Protecting Power, even by a single Power, was introduced in order to ensure that the scrutiny system would function under all circumstances.

The debates of the Diplomatic Conference and their results show that the international community has not advanced a great deal over the last three decades in the general concept of its mutual responsibility , and that by no means has it decided to advance, even to a small extent, the application of international law. Some conclusions, notably those concerning the concept of Article 5, paragraph 4 (designation of the substitute), are the result of a consensus between the Eastern bloc and Western countries in the absence of the Third World in the working group and at the time the provision was adopted. Undeniably, the adoption of this article represents a success for the Soviet Union which, moreover, considers that 'any attempt to modify this text would have unfortunate consequences'.

It is interesting to note that, despite the undeniably uniform position of the USSR and the other socialist countries with regard to questions of principle, their points of view differ and may even be termed as divergent. For example, in Poland's view, Article 5 is not wholly satisfactory and represents 'a genuine compromise between the principle of the protection of victims and that of the sovereignty of States'.

Furthermore, many delegates attending the Diplomatic Conference were concerned by the need for a scrutiny mechanism and an effective application system for the implementation of humanitarian law regulations in practice.

f) The Enquiry Commission: Thus, three amendments were submitted at the second Session of the Diplomatic Conference with a view to establishing an Enquiry Commission amendment CDDH/I/241 and Add.1 submitted by Denmark, Norway, New Zealand and Sweden; amendment CDDH/I/267 submitted by Pakistan; and amendment CDDH/I/316 submitted by Japan.

Numerous delegations welcomed an initiative aimed at resolving the enquiry system problem. Established by the Conventions of 1929 and 1949, this system had nonetheless never been applied effectively. Furthermore, the ICRC promised to assume the role of administrator and to take on certain functions aimed at appointing the Committee, but without compromising its impartiality in the investigation process itself.

This suggestion met with favourable reactions among many Third World countries. Indeed, the delegate from the Syrian Arab Republic declared that 'international humanitarian law would remain a dead letter if it did not include provisions to ensure its application and the repression of breaches'.

On the other hand, Mr. Bindschedler, delegate of Switzerland, was somewhat sceptical and expressed his reservations about the proposal. He considered the procedure for the establishment of the Commission to be too lengthy and expressed doubts as to its influence in practice.

His reservations were positively received by the socialist countries, opposed as they were to any type of obligatory mandate. Moreover, all the socialist countries considered the amendments to be unacceptable 'both for practical reasons and for reasons concerning international law' as they considered the constitution of investigative committees to be beyond the scope of the Conference. They were also opposed to the constitution of supra-national bodies which, in their view, was 'contrary to international law', in particular to the principles of non-interference in internal affairs, and a threat to sovereignty. They considered the provisions contained in the Geneva Conventions of 1949 to be satisfactory without the need for substantial modifications, since they are founded on the consent of the Parties to the conflict and take the Parties' interests into account. Thus, they expressed their preference for the obligations incumbent to the Parties, and recalled that the very causes of wars should be eliminated, thereby rendering the creation of such committees a moot point. Mr. Graefrath also pointed out that, if it is not possible to create a procedure for the regulation of litigations in time of peace, one cannot expect to resolve these problems in time of war. Consequently, he felt this task should be entrusted to the Security Council.

Thus, a number of principles may be derived from the discussions and contributions made by the socialist countries in this regard:

* the Commission's inability to establish an investigation on its own initiative;
* difficulties in safeguarding the impartiality of members of the Commission;
* the inability to take action based on the consent of one Party alone, or based on a request by the Protecting Power;
* concern over communicating the Commission's conclusions to the depositary, and particular concern over the proposal to render these conclusions public, as they 'could be distorted by the vast means of global information owing to the political orientation of most of these means'.

The socialist countries:

* draw attention to the difficulties involved in the designation of members of the Commission by the ICRC, for example, or the International Court of Justice;
* are opposed to too extensive competence;
* 'bearing in mind the differences existing between the penal systems and their varying requirements for proof, it is difficult to see how it would be possible to appreciate the value of the proof submitted'.

g) The International Fact-Finding Commission: During the course of the debates, the delegate of Egypt expressed the centre line, thereby satisfying not only those favouring the development of an effective enquiry system, but also the sceptics and even the opposers of development in this domain. The line of compromise is apparent in his speech and resulted in the adoption of Article

90 of Protocol I and the creation of the International Fact-Finding Commission.

h) Reprisals: Draft Protocol I and its final version contain several provisions prohibiting reprisals (Articles 51 to 56). These provisions were supported by all the socialist countries. Poland even took a step further and proposed the general prohibition of reprisals although this proposal was opposed by a number of countries. France, in particular, had proposed a provision allowing for exceptions and specifying particular conditions in which the Party to the conflict could have recourse to reprisals. The socialist countries saw this French proposal as a step back from the Geneva Conventions of 1949. In their view, a provision of this nature would result in the law of retaliation and would jeopardize the very foundations of international humanitarian law. The two amendments proposed by France and Poland were finally withdrawn by their authors since it was most unlikely that a consensus for a general provision in this regard would be obtained.

i) Repression of violations and the superior order: Since World War II and during the Diplomatic Conferences of 1949 and 1974-1977, the socialist countries actively supported the development of provisions concerning the repression of violations of international humanitarian law. Although they obtained satisfaction in most cases, no solution was found with respect to the superior order. Article 77 of draft Protocol I, affirming that no-one shall be punished for refusal to obey an order which would constitute a grave breach, and non-exoneration in cases where the accused acted on orders from his government or his superior, was not adopted during the Plenary Session of the Conference. The socialist countries supporting this provision expressed their regret that the article was not adopted 'since it was founded on the principles applied at Nuremberg and later confirmed by resolutions of the General Assembly of the United Nations, which now form part of international law'. The delegate of Poland, however, affirmed that 'the principle of Nuremberg remains a very important norm of international law'. Future codification of humanitarian law will have to be awaited, therefore, before this issue can be resolved.

III Conclusions

It seems likely that the issues to which no solution was found during the Diplomatic Conference of 1974-1977 will remain unresolved in the near future. The changes which have occurred in the international community since 1977 will certainly not facilitate the search for new legislative solutions.

If the content of international humanitarian law is to be improved upon, the Additional Protocols will have to be ratified or adhered to. This is an enormous task in itself. There is no doubt that ratification of the Protocols by the socialist countries will depend on the attitude adopted by the United States and other NATO countries. As soon as such ratification appears likely, the socialist countries will advance, even rapidly, towards ratification.

Yet, perfect legal instruments alone are not sufficient. Their dissemination and application must also be ensured. Over the years, the ICRC has widely developed a dissemination programme for humanitarian law but, to date, it has hardly touched one of the most important targets: the armies of the Warsaw Pact countries.

New avenues must thus be explored in this respect. Activities for the dissemination of international humanitarian law are still limited. A common declaration by the Warsaw pact and NATO countries concerning the promotion of knowledge and the application of international humanitarian law—particularly the Geneva Conventions of 1949, which were ratified by all such States—should, surely, be possible. A declaration of this kind on a non-controversial point could serve a useful purpose in the search for a political basis for the development of dissemination in socialist countries.

In its present state, humanitarian law represents a great complex of legal norms, and the interpretation of its numerous provisions constitutes a task which even lawyers specializing in this subject find difficult to achieve. It is, therefore, difficult to imagine a soldier or even an officer having a proper understanding of the subject. Consequently, it is desirable that the fundamental principles of humanitarian law be identified for those called upon to apply the law in the battlefield. Requests for the identification of these principles in a simplified form acceptable to all parties were formulated during and after the Diplomatic Conference. As a result, an attempt in this respect was made through the adoption of the fundamental principles by one of the Round Table meetings of the Institute of Humanitarian Law at San Remo. An important contribution could be made by the Independent Commission were it to submit a draft of these fundamental principles to the international community. A draft of this nature could then be adopted by an International Conference of the Red Cross or by the General Assembly of the United Nations in the form of a Declaration. This would constitute a significant step towards the application of international humanitarian law in potential conflicts.

It should be stressed that the application of humanitarian law by the socialist countries depends—more so than for other countries—on the evaluation of political interests. If the application of humanitarian law (both with regard to its effects and its propagandist character) is seen as serving the interests of its 'final cause', the Soviet Union would not hesitate to develop, affirm and apply the law. But it would willingly abandon the application of the law if it represented an obstacle to the realization of its fundamental objectives. Thus, although the non-communist world considers the two basic principles of the laws of armed conflict (i.e. the principle of humanity and the principle of military necessity) to be antagonistic, in the view of Marxist and Soviet philosophy the two principles are not opposed. Quite the contrary, the two principles are not only consistent, but tend towards an identical aim, running parallel with or as an alternative to the realization of their final objective.

Notes

1. A.I. Poltorak, L.I. Savinskii. *Vooruzhennye Konflikty I Mezhdunarodnoe Pravo*. Moskow, Nauka, 1976, p. 80.

Appendix I:
List of States Party to the Additional Protocols on 31.5.86

Protocol I	Date[1]	R/A[2]	Protocol II
46. Angola	(20.9.1984	— A)	
25. Austria[3]	(13.8.1982	— R)	22. Austria[3]
14. Bahamas	(10.4.1980	— A)	13. Bahamas
16. Bangladesh	(8.9.1980	— A)	15. Bangladesh
58. Belgium	(20.5.1986	— R)	51. Belgium
42. Belize	(29.6.1984	— A)	36. Belize
59. Benin	(28.5.1986	— A)	52. Benin
37. Bolivia	(8.12.1983	— A)	30. Bolivia
6. Botswana	(23.5.1979	— A)	6. Botswana
39. Cameroon	(16.3.1984	— A)	33. Cameroon
44. Central African Republic	(17.7.1984	— A)	38. Central African Republic
33. China	(14.9.1983	— A)	27. China
52. Comoros	(21.11.1985	— A)	45. Comoros
35. Congo	(10.11.1983	— A)	29. Congo
38. Costa Rica	(15.12.1983	— A)	31. Costa Rica
27. Cuba	(25.11.1982	— A)	
7. Cyprus	(1.6.1979	— R)	
24. Denmark[3]	(17.6.1982	— R)	21. Denmark[3]
4. Ecuador	(10.4.1979	— R)	4. Ecuador
3. El Salvador	(23.11.1978	— R)	3. El Salvador
15. Finland[3]	(7.8.1980	— R)	14. Finland[3]
	(24.2.1984	— A)	32. France
13. Gabon	(8.4.1980	— A)	12. Gabon
1. Ghana	(28.2.1978	— R)	1. Ghana
43. Guinea	(11.7.1984	— A)	37. Guinea
53. Holy See	(21.11.1985	— R)	46. Holy See
57. Italy[3]	(27.2.1986	— R)	50. Italy[3]
5. Jordan	(1.5.1979	— R)	5. Jordan
20. Korea (Rep)	(15.1.1982	— R)	18. Korea (Rep)
49. Kuwait	(17.1.1985	— A)	42. Kuwait
17. Laos	(18.11.1980	— R)	16. Laos
2. Libya	(7.6.1978	— A)	2. Libya
12. Mauritania	(14.3.1980	— A)	11. Mauritania

22. Mauritius	(22.3.1982 — A)	20. Mauritius
30. Mexico	(10.3.1983 — A)	
31. Mozambique	(14.3.1983 — A)	
34. Namibia	(18.10.1983 — A)	28. Namibia
8. Niger	(8.6.1979 — R)	7. Niger
19. Norway[3]	(14.12.1981 — R)	17. Norway[3]
40. Oman	(29.3.1984 — A)	34. Oman
48. Rwanda	(19.11.1984 — A)	41. Rwanda
56. St. Christopher and Nevis	(14.2.1986 — A)	49. St. Christopher and Nevis
26. St. Lucia	(7.10.1982 — A)	23. St. Lucia
32. St. Vincent and the Grenadines	(8.4.1983 — A)	26. St. Vincent and the Grenadines
51. Senegal	(7.5.1985 — R)	44. Senegal
47. Seychelles	(8.11.1984 — A)	40. Seychelles
55. Surinam	(16.12.1985 — A)	48. Surinam
11. Sweden[3]	(31.8.1979 — R)	10. Sweden[3]
21. Switzerland[3]	(17.2.1982 — R)	19. Switzerland[3]
36. Syria	(14.11.1983 — A)	
28. Tanzania	(15.2.1983 — A)	24. Tanzania
41. Togo	(21.6.1984 — R)	35. Togo
10. Tunisia	(9.8.1979 — R)	9. Tunisia
29. United Arab Emirates	(9.3.1983 — A)	25. United Arab Emirates
54. Uruguay	(13.12.1985 — A)	47. Uruguay
50. Vanuatu	(28.2.1985 — A)	43. Vanuatu
18. Viet Nam	(19.10.1981 — R)	
45. Western Samoa	(23.8.1984 — A)	39. Western Samoa
9. Yugoslavia	(11.6.1979 — R)	8. Yugoslavia
23. Zaire	(3.6.1982 — A)	

Total number of States party:
  Protocol I : 59
  Protocol II : 52

1. Date when instrument of ratification/accession was deposited.
2. R: Ratification   A: Accession
3. Declaration provided for under Article 90 of Protocol I.

The numbers preceding the names of the countries show the chronological order of ratification or accession.

Appendix II: Memorandum
Request for accession to the Protocols Additional to the Geneva Conventions of 1949 (8th June 1985)

'In view of the increasing dangers threatening the civilian population in contemporary armed conflicts and of the need to protect all the victims of such conflicts, it is incumbent on the international community to ensure respect for fundamental humanitarian norms in all circumstances.

The Independent Commission urges all States to accede to the humanitarian instruments to which they are not yet Parties and to comply with all the provisions of such instruments.

In particular it calls upon States to ratify, or accede to, the Protocols Additional to the 1949 Geneva Conventions adopted on 8 June 1977. These Protocols are the result of the most recent common effort in the development of humanitarian law to ensure better legal protection of all victims of armed conflicts. A call for ratification or accession is all the more justified in the present international context where international peace and security is threatened by the armed conflicts going on in several parts of the world.

Although the 1977 Protocols bring about a substantial improvement in the protection of victims of armed conflicts, all the rules included in them are not new. They develop and adapt to the conditions of contemporary armed conflicts the existing customary or treaty law, inter alia, the 1949 Geneva Conventions and the 1907 Hague Regulations.

The ratification of Protocol I of 1977 would therefore not imply State acceptance of any new rules restricting the choice of the means of warfare, which is already restricted by customary law and by conventional instruments previously acceded to. Essentially, the Protocol merely specifies and reformulates those restrictions in the present context, while at the same time considerably improving the protection of the civilian population.

Protocol II develops and adds to the basic guarantees contained in common Article 3 of the Geneva Conventions. It therefore brings about a considerable improvement in the protection of victims of internal conflicts. Its scope is restricted to what are clearly civil wars where dissident armed forces have a territorial base. Therefore, beyond the general humanitarian interest in sparing the civilian population, considerations of reciprocity imply that it is in the interest of all to follow those rules.

Both Additional Protocols to the Geneva Conventions were adopted by consensus at a Conference attended by nearly all States which reached a fundamental agreement on important principles. The 1977 consensus should now find expression in the ratification of those instruments by all States, so that the Protocols are as universally accepted as the 1949 Geneva Conventions.

The ratification of these instruments is part of the current efforts to promote a climate of confidence and security at the regional and international level.'

Appendix III:
Declaration of Fundamental Rights of the Individual in Time of Internal Disturbances or Public Emergency (ICRC)*

1. No one shall be subjected to torture or to inhuman or degrading punishments or treatments;
2. No one shall be punished for an infraction he has not committed;
3. No one shall be condemned for any act or omission which, at the time when it was committed, did not constitute a criminal offence under national or international law;
4. No sentence shall be passed or execution carried out without previous judgment pronounced by a regularly constituted court affording all the judicial guarantees which are recognized as indispensable by civilized peoples;
5. Any person deprived of liberty due to such events shall at all times be accorded human treatment in conformity with the Standard Minimum Rules for the Treatment of Prisoners, as established by the United Nations Organization;

* Conference of government experts, 1971, No. V, p.86.

When constitutional guarantees have been suspended, and in particular when, due to the events, these persons are imprisoned for an indeterminate time and without being indicted or brought before a court, an impartial humanitarian institution such as the ICRC shall be authorized to visit them;

6. Collective penalties, taking of hostages, measures of reprisal against persons and their property are prohibited;

7. The wounded and sick shall be collected and cared for in all circumstances;

   The national Societies of the Red Cross shall at all times be authorized to carry on their relief activities on behalf of the victims of situations of internal disturbances;

8. An impartial humanitarian body, such as the ICRC, may at all times, offer its services, on behalf of all the victims, to the authorities in power;

   Neither this offer, nor its acceptance, shall have any effect on the legal status of the persons involved in these situations of internal disturbances.

Appendix IV:

Resolution 32/64, as recommended by Third Committee, A/32/355, adopted without vote by Assembly on 8 December 1977, meeting 98.

The General Assembly,

Bearing in mind that the principles proclaimed in the Charter of the United Nations concerning the dignity and worth of the human person place upon Member States the obligation to promote universal respect for, and observance of, human rights and fundamental freedoms for all,

Recalling article 5 of the Universal Declaration of Human Rights and article 7 of the International Covenant on Civil and Political Rights, which stipulate that no one shall be subjected to torture or to cruel, inhuman or degrading treatment or punishment,

Recalling also the Declaration on the Protection of All Persons from Being Subjected to Torture and Other Cruel, Inhuman or Degrading Treatment or Punishment, unanimously adopted by its resolution 3452(XXX) of 9 December 1975, as well as its resolution 31/85 of 13 December 1976,

Recognizing the necessity for further international action in the form of a convention for the elimination of torture and other cruel, inhuman or degrading treatment or punishment,

Recognizing also the importance of action by Member States to develop and utilize their national machinery to eliminate torture and other cruel, inhuman or degrading treatment or punishment,

1. Calls upon all Member States to reinforce their support of the Declaration on the Protection of All Persons from Being Subjected to Torture and Other Cruel, Inhuman or Degrading Treatment or Punishment by making unilateral declarations against torture and other cruel, inhuman or degrading treatment or punishment, along the lines of the text which is annexed to the present resolution, and depositing them with the Secretary-General;

2. Urges all Member States to give maximum publicity to their unilateral declarations against torture and other cruel, inhuman or degrading treatment or punishment;

3. Requests the Secretary-General to inform the General Assembly, in annual reports, of such unilateral declarations against torture and other cruel, inhuman or degrading treatment or punishment as may be deposited by Member States.

ANNEX

Model unilateral declaration against torture and other cruel, inhuman or degrading treatment or punishment

The Government of . . . .hereby declares its intention:

(a) To comply with the Declaration on the Protection of All Persons from Being Subjected to Torture and Other Cruel, Inhuman or Degrading Treatment or Punishment (General Assembly resolution 3452(XXX), annex);

(b) To implement, through legislation and other effective measures, the provisions of the said Declaration.

Appendix V:

Resolution 3452(XXX), annexing Declaration, as recommended by Third Committee, A/10408, adopted without vote by Assembly on 9 December 1975, meeting 2433.

The General Assembly,

Considering that, in accordance with the principles proclaimed in the Charter of the United Nations, recognition of the inherent dignity and of the equal and inalienable rights of all members of the human family is the foundation of freedom, justice and peace in that world,

Considering that these rights derive from the inherent dignity of the human person,

Considering also the obligation of States under the Charter, in particular Article 55, to promote universal respect for, and observance of, human rights and fundamental freedoms,

Having regard to article 5 of the Universal Declaration of Human Rights and article 7 of the International Covenant on Civil and Political Rights, both of which provide that no one may be subjected to torture or to cruel, inhuman or degrading treatment or punishment,

Adopts the Declaration on the Protection of All Persons from Being Subjected to Torture and Other Cruel, Inhuman or Degrading Treatment or Punishment, the text of which is annexed to the present resolution, as a guideline for all States and other entities exercising effective power.

ANNEX

Declaration on the Protection of All Persons from Being Subjected to Torture and Other Cruel, Inhuman or Degrading Treatment or Punishment

Article 1

1. For the purpose of this Declaration, torture means any act by

which severe pain or suffering, whether physical or mental, is intentionally inflicted by or at the instigation of a public official on a person for such purposes as obtaining from him or a third person information or confession, punishing him for an act he has committed or is suspected of having committed, or intimidating him or other persons. It does not include pain or suffering arising only from, inherent in or incidental to, lawful sanctions to the extent consistent with the Standard Minimum Rules for the Treatment of Prisoners.

2. Torture constitutes an aggravated and deliberate form of cruel, inhuman or degrading treatment or punishment.

Article 2
Any act of torture or other cruel, inhuman or degrading treatment or punishment is an offence to human dignity and shall be condemned as a denial of the purposes of the Charter of the United Nations and as a violation of the human rights and fundamental freedoms proclaimed in the Universal Declaration of Human Rights.

Article 3
No State may permit or tolerate torture or other cruel, inhuman or degrading treatment or punishment. Exceptional circumstances such as a state of war or a threat of war, internal political instability or any other public emergency may not be invoked as a justification of torture or other cruel, inhuman or degrading treatment or punishment.

Article 4
Each State shall, in accordance with the provisions of this Declaration, take effective measures to prevent torture and other cruel, inhuman or degrading treatment or punishment from being practised within its jurisdiction.

Article 5
The training of law enforcement personnel and of other public officials who may be responsible for persons deprived of their liberty shall ensure that full account is taken of the prohibition against torture and other cruel, inhuman or degrading treatment or punishment. This prohibition shall also, where appropriate, be

included in such general rules or instructions as are issued in regard to the duties and functions of anyone who may be involved in the custody or treatment of such persons.

Article 6
Each State shall keep under systematic review interrogation methods and practices as well as arrangements for the custody and treatment of persons deprived of their liberty in its territory, with a view to preventing any cases of torture or other cruel, inhuman or degrading treatment or punishment.

Article 7
Each State shall ensure that all acts of torture as defined in article 1 are offences under its criminal law. The same shall apply in regard to acts which constitute participation in, complicity in, incitement to or an attempt to commit torture.

Article 8
Any person who alleges that he has been subjected to torture or other cruel, inhuman or degrading treatment or punishment by or at the instigation of a public official shall have the right to complain to, and to have his case impartially examined by, the competent authorities of the State concerned.

Article 9
Wherever there is reasonable ground to believe that an act of torture as defined in article 1 has been committed, the competent authorities of the State concerned shall promptly proceed to an impartial investigation even if there has been no formal complaint.

Article 10
If an investigation under article 8 or article 9 establishes that an act of torture as defined in article 1 appears to have been committed, criminal proceedings shall be instituted against the alleged offender or offenders in accordance with national law. If an allegation of other forms of cruel, inhuman or degrading treatment or punishment is considered to be well founded, the alleged offender or offenders shall be subject to criminal, disciplinary or other appropriate proceedings.

Article 11
Where it is proved that an act of torture or other cruel, inhuman or degrading treatment or punishment has been committed by or at the instigation of a public official, the victim shall be afforded redress and compensation in accordance with national law.

Article 12
Any statement which is established to have been made as a result of torture or other cruel, inhuman or degrading treatment or punishment may not be invoked as evidence against the person concerned or against any other person in any proceedings.

Appendix VI:
Resolution 2444(XXIII), as recommended by Third Committee, A/7433, adopted by Assembly unanimously (111-0) on 19 December 1968, meeting 1748.

The General Assembly,

Recognizing the necessity of applying basic humanitarian principles in all armed conflicts,

Taking note of resolution XXIII on human rights in armed conflicts, adopted on 12 May 1968 by the International Conference on Human Rights,

Affirming that the provisions of that resolution need to be implemented effectively as soon as possible,

1. Affirms resolution XXVIII of the XXth International Conference of the Red Cross held at Vienna in 1965, which laid down, *inter alia*, the following principles for observance by all governmental and other authorities responsible for action in armed conflicts:

(a) That the right of the parties to a conflict to adopt means of injuring the enemy is not unlimited;

(b) That it is prohibited to launch attacks against the civilian populations as such;

(c) That distinction must be made at all times between persons taking part in the hostilities and members of the civilian population to the effect that the latter be spared as much as possible;

2. Invites the Secretary-General, in consultation with the International Committee of the Red Cross and other appropriate international organizations, to study:

(a) Steps which could be taken to secure the better application of existing humanitarian international conventions and rules in all armed conflicts;

(b) The need for additional humanitarian international conventions or for other appropriate legal instruments to ensure the better protection of civilians, prisoners and combatants in all armed conflicts and the prohibition and limitation of the use of certain methods and means of warfare;

3. Requests the Secretary-General to take all other necessary steps to give effect to the provisions of the present resolution and to report to the General Assembly at its twenty-fourth session on the steps he has taken;

4. Further requests Member States to extend all possible assistance to the Secretary-General in the preparation of the study requested in paragraph 2 above;

5. Calls upon all States which have not yet done so to become parties to the Hague Conventions of 1899 and 1907, the Geneva Protocol of 1925 and the Geneva Conventions of 1949.

Appendix VII:

Resolution 2675(XXV), as recommended by Third Committee, A/8178, adopted by Assembly on 9 December 1970, meeting 1922, by 109 votes to 0, with 8 abstentions.

The General Assembly,

Noting that in the present century the international community has accepted an increased role and new responsibilities for the alleviation of human suffering in any form and in particular during armed conflicts,

Recalling that to this end a series of international instruments has

been adopted, including the four Geneva Conventions of 1949,
Recalling further its resolution 2444(XXIII) of 19 December 1968
on respect for human rights in armed conflicts,

Bearing in mind the need for measures to ensure the better protection of human rights in armed conflicts of all types,

Noting with appreciation the work that is being undertaken in this respect by the International Committee of the Red Cross,

Noting with appreciation the reports of the Secretary-General on respect for human rights in armed conflicts,

Convinced that civilian populations are in special need of increased protection in time of armed conflicts,

Recognizing the importance of the strict application of the Geneva Convention relative to the Protection of Civilian Persons in Time of War, of 12 August 1949,

Affirms the following basic principles for the protection of civilian populations in armed conflicts, without prejudice to their future elaboration within the framework of progressive development of the international law of armed conflict:

1. Fundamental human rights, as accepted in international law and laid down in international instruments, continue to apply fully in situations of armed conflict.

2. In the conduct of military operations during armed conflicts, a distinction must be made at all times between persons actively taking part in the hostilities and civilian populations.

3. In the conduct of military operations, every effort should be made to spare civilian populations from the ravages of war, and all necessary precautions should be taken to avoid injury, loss or damage to civilian populations.

4. Civilian populations as such should not be the object of military operations.

5. Dwellings and other installations that are used only by civilian populations should not be the object of military operations.

6. Places or areas designated for the sole protection of civilians, such as hospital zones or similar refuges, should not be the object of military operations.

7. Civilian populations, or individual members thereof, should not be the object of reprisals, forcible transfers or other assaults on their integrity.

8. The provision of international relief to civilian populations is in conformity with the humanitarian principles of the Charter

of the United Nations, the Universal Declaration of Human Rights and other international instruments in the field of human rights. The Declaration of Principles for International Humanitarian Relief to the Civilian Population in Disaster Situations, as laid down in resolution XXVI adopted by the twenty-first International Conference of the Red Cross, shall apply in situations of armed conflict, and all parties to a conflict should make every effort to facilitate this application.

Appendix VIII:
Information note on the Independent Commission on International Humanitarian Issues

The establishment of an Independent Commission on International Humanitarian Issues is the response of a group of eminent persons from all parts of the world to the need to enhance international awareness of humanitarian issues and to promote a climate favouring progress in the humanitarian field.

The Independent Commission on International Humanitarian Issues held its first plenary meeting in New York in November 1983. Its work is intended to be a part of the continuing search by the world community for a more adequate international framework to uphold human dignity and rise to the challenge of colossal injustices and humanitarian problems arising with increasing frequency in a modern world more commonly concerned with economic, political and military priorities.

Background
In 1981, the United Nations General Assembly adopted a resolution relating to a New International Humanitarian Order in which it recognized: 'the importance of further improving a comprehensive international framework which takes fully into account existing instruments relating to humanitarian questions as well as the need for addressing those aspects which are not yet adequately covered.' It was stressed that 'institutional arrangements and actions of

governmental and non-governmental bodies might need to be further strengthened to respond effectively in situations requiring humanitarian actions.'

The following year, the General Assembly lent its support to the 'proposal for establishment, outside the United Nations framework, of an "Independent Commission on International Humanitarian Issues" composed of leading personalities in the humanitarian field or having wide experience of government or world affairs.'

In 1985, the United Nations Secretary-General presented to the General Assembly a comprehensive report and comments from governments on the New International Humanitarian Order. The report included a description of the Independent Commission and its work. In a subsequent resolution, the General Assembly took note of the activities of the Commission and looked forward to the outcome of its efforts and its Final Report.

Composition of the Commission

The Commission is an independent body whose members participate in their personal capacity and not as representatives of governments or international bodies to which they may belong. Its work is intended to complement, not to duplicate, work being done by existing governmental or non-governmental bodies, and to assist, not to interfere with, governmental negotiations or inter-state relations.

The composition of the Commission, which is intended to remain limited, is based on equitable geographical distribution. At present, it has twenty-seven members. The Commission operates through a small Secretariat which coordinates research activities and provides support services for its work. In its deliberations, the Commission benefits from the advice of governments, existing international governmental and non-governmental bodies and leading experts.

Programme of Work

There are, of course, many important subjects relating to humanitarian issues of relevance to contemporary society. With a limited mandate of three years, 1983-1986, the Commission has chosen three main areas of study, in which it feels its contribution can be particularly effective. These are:

* Humanitarian norms in the context of armed conflicts.
* Natural and man-made disasters.
* Vulnerable groups requiring special care and protection such as refugees and displaced persons, stateless persons, children and youth, indigenous populations, etc.

The conclusions and recommendations of the Commission are based on studies carried out with the help of recognized experts and national or international bodies chosen from all parts of the world for their specialized knowledge or experience. In addition to direct input by experts in the form of policy-oriented research papers, the Commission also sponsors panel discussions or brainstorming sessions. In order to avoid duplication of effort, complement ongoing projects and help promote innovative solutions, the Commission works closely with agencies already involved in dealing with these issues. Heads of these organizations or their representatives are invited to the Commission's bi-annual plenary meetings.

Studies and expert advice received by the Commission as well as its own delibertions on various issues are reflected in a series of sectoral reports which are published from time to time. These reports are addressed to policy-makers within governments, regional bodies, inter-governmental and non-governmental organizations and the general public. They are intended to be readable summaries of the subject, presenting an overview of the situation, prompting further research, making recommendations and suggesting concrete options for follow-up action.

The first sectoral report for the Commission, entitled *Famine: A Man-Made Disaster?* was published in 1985. The purpose of this Report was to increase public awareness of the famine conditions afflicting much of Africa and the Third World, recommend positive solutions and facilitate further study and analysis of the situation. The Report has already been published in eight languages, and the Commission feels that rather than waiting for the publication of its Final Report, the dissemination of these sectoral reports is a worthwhile exercise.

Sectoral reports on Deforestation, Desertification, Disappeared Persons, Street Children, Humanitarian Norms and Armed Conflict, and Refugees have been published in 1986. Additional reports on Indigenous Peoples, Statelessness, Mass Expulsions, Disaster

Management, Urban Migration and other topics are forthcoming.

The Commission's work will culminate in the publication of its Final Report scheduled at the end of 1986. The Final Report will address the humanitarian implications of a diverse range of global issues. It will be a policy and practice-oriented blueprint for effective response to the tremendous challenge posed by humanitarian problems in modern society.

Members of the Commission

Sadruddin AGA KHAN (Iran) — UN High Commissioner for Refugees, 1965-77; Special Consultant to the UN Secretary General since 1978. Special Rapporteur of the UN Human Rights Commission, 1981. Founder-President of the Bellerive Group.

Susanna AGNELLI (Italy) — Under-Secretary of State for Foreign Affairs since 1983. Member of the Italian Senate. Member of the European Parliament, 1979-81. Journalist and author.

Talal Bin Abdul Aziz AL SAUD (Saudi Arabia) — President, the Arab Gulf Programme for UN Development Organizations (AGFUND). UNICEF's Special Envoy, 1980-84. Former Administrator of Royal Palaces, Minister of Communications, of Finance and National Economy, and Vice-President of the Supreme Planning Commission.

Paulo Evaristo ARNS (Brazil) — Cardinal Archbishop of Sao Paulo. Chancellor of the Pontifical Catholic University, Sao Paulo State. Journalist and author.

Mohammed BEDJAOUI (Algeria) — Judge at the International Court of Justice since 1982. Secretary-General, Council of Ministers, 1962-64; Minister of Justice, 1964-70. Ambassador to France, 1970-79; UNESCO, 1971-79; and the United Nations in New York, 1979-82.

Henrik BEER (Sweden) — Secretary-General of the League of Red Cross Societies, 1960-82; Secretary-General of the Swedish

Red Cross, 1947-60. Member of the International Institute for Environment and Development and the International Institute of Humanitarian Law.

Luis ECHEVERRIA ALVAREZ (Mexico) — President of the Republic, 1970-76; Founder and Director-General of the Centre for Economic and Social Studies of the Third World since 1976. Former Ambassador to Australia, New Zealand and UNESCO.

Pierre GRABER (Switzerland) — President of the Swiss Confederation, 1975; Foreign Minister, 1975-78. President of the Diplomatic Conference on Humanitarian Law, 1974-77.

Ivan L. HEAD (Canada) — President of the International Development Research Centre (IDRC). Special Assistant to the Prime Minister of Canada, 1968-78. Queen's Counsel.

M. HIDAYATULLAH (India) — Vice-President of India, 1979-84. Chief Justice of the Supreme Court, 1968-70; Chief Justice of the Nagpur and Madhya Pradesh High Courts, 1954-58; Chancellor of the Jamia Millia Islamia since 1979. Former Chancellor of the Universities of Delhi, Punjab. Author

Aziza HUSSEIN (Egypt) — Member of the Population Council. President of the International Planned Parenthood Federation, 1977-85. Fellow at the International Peace Academy, Helsinki, 1971; the Aspen Institute of Humanistic Studies, 1978-79.

Manfred LACHS (Poland) — Judge at the International Court of Justice since 1967 and its President, 1973-76. Professor of Political Science and International Law. Former Chairman of the UN Legal Committee on the Peaceful Uses of Outer Space.

Robert S. McNAMARA (USA) — President of the World Bank, 1968-81; Secretary of Defense, 1961-68. President, Ford Motor Company, 1960-61; Trustee of the Brookings Institute, Ford Foundation, the Urban Institute and the California Institute of Technology. Author.

Lazar MOJSOV (Yugoslavia) — Member of the Presidency of

the Socialist Federal Republic of Yugoslavia. Former Foreign Minister. Ambassador to the USSR, Mongolia, Austria, the United Nations, 1958-74. President of the UN General Assembly, 32nd Session and of the Special Session on Disarmament, 1978.

Mohammed MZALI (Tunisia) — Prime Minister and General Secretary of the Destorian Socialist Party. Member of the National Assembly since 1959. Former Minister of National Defence, Education, Youth and Sports and Health. Author.

Sadako OGATA (Japan) — Professor at the Institute of International Relations, Sophia University, Tokyo. Representative of Japan to the United Nations Human Rights Commission. Member of the Trilateral Commission.

David OWEN (United Kingdom) — Member of Parliament since 1966. Leader of the Social Democratic Party since 1983. Foreign Secretary, 1977-79.

Willibald P. PAHR (Austria) — Secretary-General of the World Tourism Organization. Federal Minister of Foreign Affairs, 1976-83. Ambassador. Vice-President of the International Institute of Human Rights (Strasbourg).

Shridath S. RAMPHAL (Guyana) — Secretary-General of the Commonwealth since 1975. Former Attorney-General, Foreign Minister and Minister of Justice.

RU XIN (China) — Vice-President of the Chinese Academy of Social Sciences. Professor of Philosophy at the Xiamen University. Executive President of the Chinese National Society of the History of World Philosophies.

Salim A. SALIM (Tanzania) — Deputy Prime Minister and Minister of Defence. Former Prime Minister and Foreign Minister. Ambassador to Egypt, India, China and Permanent Representative to the United Nations. Former President of the UN General Assembly and the Security Council.

Léopold Sédar SENGHOR (Senegal) — Member of the French

Academy. President of the Republic of Senegal, 1960-80. Cabinet Minister in the French Government before leading his country to independence in 1960. Poet and philosopher.

SOEDJATMOKO (Indonesia) — Rector of the United Nations University, Tokyo since 1980. Ambassador to the United States. Member of the Club of Rome and Trustee of the Aspen Institute and the Ford Foundation.

Hassan bin TALAL (Jordan) — Crown Prince of the Hashemite Kingdom. Founder of the Royal Scientific Society and the Arab Thought Forum. Concerned with development planning and the formulation of national, economic and social policies. Author.

Desmond TUTU (South Africa) — Archbishop of Cape Town. Winner of Nobel Peace Prize. Former Secretary-General of the South African Council of Churches. Professor of Theology.

Simone VEIL (France) — Member of the European Parliament and its President 1979-82; chairs the Legal Affairs Committee of the European Parliament. Former Minister of Health, Social Security and Family Affairs, 1974-79.

E. Gough WHITLAM (Australia) — Prime Minister, 1972-75; Minister of Foreign Affairs, 1972-73; Member of Parliament, 1952-78. Ambassador to UNESCO.